THE DIARY OF ANNE FRANK
NOTES

including
- *Introduction*
- *Historical Background*
- *List of Characters*
- *Critical Commentaries*
    The First Year
    The Second Year
- *Character Backgrounds and Fates*
    Anne Frank
    Margot Frank
    Otto Frank
    Mrs. Frank
    The Van Daans
    Mr. Düssel
    The Dutch "Protectors"
    Lies
- *Essay Topics*
- *Selected Bibliography*

by
Dorothea Shefer-Vanson, M.A.
Hebrew University of Jerusalem

D1726531

INCORPORATED

LINCOLN, NEBRASKA 68501

THE DIARY OF ANNE FRANK
Notes

". . . ideals, dreams, and
cherished hopes rise within us
only to meet the horrible truth
and be shattered . . . yet in
spite of everything I still believe
that people are really good at heart."

Anne Frank
July 15, 1944

INTRODUCTION

Anne Frank's *Diary* is not a novel or a tale of the imagination. It is the diary kept by a young Jewish girl for the two years she was forced to remain in hiding by the Nazi persecution of the Jews of Europe. Between June 1942 and August 1944, from Anne's thirteenth birthday until shortly after her fifteenth birthday, Anne Frank recorded her feelings, her emotions, and her thoughts, as well as the events that happened to her, in the diary which her father had given her as a birthday present. Together with her parents and her sister, Margot, the Van Daan family (consisting of a husband, a wife, and a son, Peter, two years older than Anne) and, later on, an elderly dentist named Mr. Düssel, Anne lived in a set of rooms at the top of an old warehouse in Amsterdam, Holland, concealed behind a hidden door and a bookcase. During the day, when people worked in the office and in the warehouse below, Anne and the others had to keep very quiet, but at night they could move around more freely, though of course they could not turn on any lights nor show in any way that the house was inhabited.

The *Diary* is many things at one and the same time. It is an amusing, enlightening, and often moving account of the *process of adolescence,* as Anne describes her thoughts and feelings about herself and the people around her, the world at large, and life in general. It is an accurate record of the way a young girl grows up and matures, in the very special circumstances in which Anne found herself throughout the two years during which she was in hiding. And it is also a vividly terrifying description of *what it was like to be a Jew* — and in hiding — at a time when the Nazis sought to kill *all* the Jews of Europe.

Above all, Anne was an ordinary girl, growing up, and eventually dying, but she was an *ordinary* girl growing up in *extraordinary* times. She loved life and laughter, was interested in history and movie stars, Greek mythology, and cats, writing, and boys. In the few entries which she wrote before the family went into hiding, we discover something of the world of a child growing up in Holland in 1942. Anne went to school, had girl friends and boyfriends, went to parties and to ice-cream parlors, rode her bike, and *chattered* (an understatement) in class. In fact, Anne chattered so much that, as a punishment for her talkativeness, she had to write several essays on the subject of "A Chatterbox." Much of this chatty quality of hers, however, spills over onto the pages of her diary, where we often feel as if she is a good friend who is confiding in us. Although the world of that period is divided from us by more than mere years, Anne's voice is very contemporary, and many of her thoughts and problems are very much like those of any youngster growing up both then and now.

Anne Frank did *not* survive the concentration camps to which she was sent after her little group was discovered. Of all the eight people who hid in the "Secret Annexe" in Amsterdam, only Anne's father survived. The pages of Anne's diary, which the Nazis left scattered on the floor when they arrested the group in hiding, were kept by the two young women who had worked in the office and had faithfully supplied the little group with food and other provisions. When Mr. Frank returned after the war, they gave him the pages of Anne's diary, and he eventually published them. And so, although Anne died, as the Nazis had intended, her spirit lives on, through her *Diary*, stronger and clearer by far than any brute force or blind hatred.

HISTORICAL BACKGROUND

The events recounted in Anne Frank's diary take place during World War II, in which almost all the countries of Europe, as well as the U.S.A. and Japan, were involved to a greater or lesser extent between 1939 and 1945. The reasons for the war are many and varied, and even the historians are not fully in agreement as to the precise causes, some blaming the harsh conditions and economic penalties imposed on Germany after its defeat in World War I, others claiming that it was the weakness of the European countries after Hitler's rise to power in Germany that was the indirect cause. All are agreed, however, that had it not been for Hitler and his policies, the war would *not* have taken place.

In addition to the various military engagements, however, the Nazis were engaged in a systematic attempt to kill off certain sections of the population – primarily Jews and Gypsies – both within Germany and in the countries which they occupied, claiming that they were "racially inferior." The murder of mentally retarded and psychologically disturbed people, as well as homosexuals, was also official Nazi policy. In some cases, these people were made to work as slaves before they were killed, so that the Germans could benefit as much as possible from their labor. To implement this scheme, the Germans established huge "concentration camps," or death camps, throughout Europe. Jews and other people were sent there in cattle trains, and upon arrival, their heads were shaved and their arms were tattooed with numbers; in addition, they were stripped of their clothes and whatever possessions they still had. They were made to work and were subjected to the strictest discipline and the most inhumane conditions before they were gassed in special chambers and their bodies burned. In those parts of Europe which were occupied by the Nazis, but where these methods of killing large numbers of people had *not yet* been established, the Nazis assembled large numbers of Jews and machine-gunned them all as they stood on the edge of huge pits which they had dug themselves, or beside natural, deep ravines, as was the case at Babi Yar, in Russia. In other places, the Nazis herded all the local Jews into the synagogue and then set it on fire.

Throughout World War II, the Nazis devoted considerable thought, equipment, and manpower to the wholesale slaughter of Europe's Jewish population, and by the time the war had ended, they had succeeded in killing six million of them, two-thirds of the total number of Jews in the world.

How could it come about that one nation regarded itself as *racially superior* to another, to the extent that it felt that it was its *right* and its *duty* to kill all the members of that other nation? How could huge "factories of death," manned by thousands of people, systematically kill off millions of people in the midst of inhabited areas without anyone protesting or even knowing what was happening? How could Hitler, a homicidal maniac, become the ruler of a country whose civilization had produced some of the world's greatest thinkers, writers, composers, and statemen? In order to obtain answers to these questions, we have to go back to the nineteenth century.

Germany was not always one united country. During the Middle Ages, Germany consisted of a series of small kingdoms and principalities, often rivals, and often even at war with one another. The language which they all shared was German, but the people differed on matters of religion, so much so that these differences occasionally erupted into wars between the Catholics and the Protestants. In the mid-nineteenth century, Bismarck (the Chancellor of Prussia, the largest German state) made it his objective to unify the various German states. This he achieved by judicious policies, arranging marriages between various royal families and obtaining treaties which were mutually beneficial to the parties concerned. By the end of the nineteenth century, Germany was united under one monarch, Kaiser Wilhelm I; it possessed colonies in Africa and was ruled by an Emperor (the German term *Kaiser* is derived from the Latin word *Caesar*).

World War I, in which Germany fought against France and England, from 1914 to 1918, was largely a result of the structural weakness of many European states and the growing military and economic strength of Germany. After four years of bitter fighting, Germany was defeated, the Kaiser fled to Holland, and a peace treaty, the Treaty of Versailles, was drawn up. This stripped Germany of its foreign colonies, imposed heavy economic penalties on the country in the form of fines and disarmament, and it changed many of the borders of the countries of Europe. This policy gave rise to severe economic problems in Germany. Hunger and poverty were widespread, and galloping inflation caused prices to rise at a dizzying rate. The middle class, which had been the chief support of the German

Republic, which was established after World War I, became embittered, and many Germans longed for the old autocratic kind of government that had formerly dominated the country.

It was during the years after World War I that Adolf Hitler, a house painter who had experienced the bitterness of defeat as a soldier in the German Army, developed his ideas of the Master Aryan Race, the need to rid Germany of "inferior" peoples, such as Jews and Gypsies, and the need to expand Germany's borders and build a Germany that was militarily strong. He gathered around him a group of people who supported his ideas and used the tactics of bullying and terrorism to obtain publicity and intimidate his opponents. His National Socialist – or Nazi – party advocated the establishment of a totalitarian state, the redistribution of the nation's wealth and the provision of jobs for everybody.

Hitler used inflammatory rhetoric in his speeches, and he was able to arouse huge audiences to hysterical enthusiasm. He claimed that Germany's problems and the decline in its power were the fault of Jews and radicals, and that the German, or Aryan, race was the Master Race, the creators of all civilization, and fitted by *nature* to rule the world. In order for this Master Race to have adequate living space, *Lebensraum,* Hitler intended to expand Germany's frontiers in the East, taking from the lands of Poland, Czechoslovakia, and Russia. The inhabitants of those countries, the Slavs, were also "inferior," according to Hitler, fit only either to serve the Master Race as slaves – or to be killed.

Hitler's Nazi party, regarded initially by most Germans as merely a lunatic fringe, began to gain ground and support within Germany after the world's economic depression, which began in 1929. In the German parliament, the *Reichstag,* the Nazis were represented alongside the various other political parties. Hitler continued to fulminate against the Jews, describing them as an alien, inferior race despite their distinguished contribution to German cultural and economic life throughout many centuries. He regarded them as being responsible for all the movements which the Nazis opposed, communism, pacifism, internationalism, and Christianity, as well as being a threat to "German racial purity." The Jews, who had resided in Germany for a thousand years and constituted half a million people, a small fraction of the population, watched in horror as Hitler's party gained power throughout the country. Many believed that the political hysteria would soon pass, that the common people would soon see Hitler for what he really was, or that, once in power, Hitler would modify his extreme views. After all, they seemed to think, Germany is a civilized country; anti-Semitic riots could never happen here. They could not imagine that millions of people would be murdered for no other reason than that they were Jews.

Hitler's racial theories and nationalism had deep roots in Germany's past. The Christian tradition of anti-Semitism and Jewish responsibility for the death of Jesus also played a role in the reluctance to regard Jews as equal members of society. When, through various parliamentary maneuvers, Hitler became the Chancellor of Germany in 1933, he immediately took measures to establish an absolute, totalitarian regime. He outlawed *all* political parties other than his own, banned *all* literature that did not support his party or that was written by Jews or communists, and introduced a set of laws, the Nuremberg Race Laws, prohibiting Jews from interacting with, or marrying, Aryans. Most Germans quietly accepted Hitler's regime, and those who did not were confronted with arrests, beatings, torture, and imprisonment.

Hitler's new laws prevented Jews from holding public office, being teachers, practicing law or medicine, working in journalism or engaging in business. Jews were forbidden to employ Aryans, and Aryans were discouraged from patronizing Jewish stores. Jewish property was confiscated, collective fines were imposed on Jewish communities, and even emigration was made difficult for Jews. The countries of the world gathered at Evian, France, in 1938 to discuss ways of absorbing the Jewish population of Germany, but no country was willing to provide a home for more than a handful of Jews. The U.S. government declined to increase its immigrant quotas, and the British, who controlled Palestine, refused to allow large numbers of Jews to go there, fearing Arab opposition to this move. Even countries like Australia and Canada, with vast tracts of uninhabited land, refused to allow large numbers of Jews to enter.

After gaining power, Hitler set about rearming Germany, even though this was *strictly prohibited* by the terms of the Treaty of Versailles. In doing so, he strengthened Germany's economy, created full employment, and restored a sense of pride to the German population. The countries of Europe, however, turned a blind eye to this flagrant disregard of the Versailles Treaty, refrained from taking any action, and thereby allowed the stage to be set for Hitler's next acts.

In 1938, encouraged by the inaction of the European nations, Hitler proceeded to invade and annex, first, Austria, and then Czechoslovakia, each time assuring the world that all he wanted was "peace," and that this would be his "last demand." By the end of 1939, when Hitler was obviously preparing to adopt a similar take-over policy toward Poland, and the efforts of Chamberlain, Britain's prime minister, to find a peaceful solution had evidently failed, France and Britain declared war on Germany.

The years since 1933 that Hitler had spent rearming Germany had not been militarily paralleled by the Allies (the European countries, the United States, and Russia) so that the outbreak of World War II found Germany vastly superior in military strength. This enabled German forces to rapidly overrun Poland, Denmark, Norway, Holland, Belgium, and France within a short space of time in 1939 and 1940, so that *within less than a year,* most of Europe was occupied by Germany. The German troops were highly mobile and mechanized, strictly disciplined, and motivated by theories of national and racial superiority. Britain's island status enabled it to withstand German threats, and although it suffered considerable devastation as a result of German bombardments, its people rallied, manufacturing arms and defending its shores and skies.

Not content with being master of most of Europe, Hitler then launched an attack against Russia in June, 1941, *despite* the non-aggression pact that Hitler had signed with Stalin in 1939. For over five years, Europe was a virtual slave empire under the Nazis. The people of Europe worked long, hard hours in farms and factories, receiving little more than subsistence rations in return, and millions of people were taken to Germany to work there. In occupied countries, any resistance was crushed ruthlessly; hostages were executed in retaliation for the killing of a single Nazi soldier, listening to British broadcasts, or possessing anti-Nazi literature were all made punishable by death. Harboring Jews was punishable either by death or by being sent to a concentration camp.

The Nazis were as efficient in setting up the machinery of death as they were in manufacturing arms. Over the years, they perfected a system of obtaining lists of *all* the Jewish inhabitants of a particular place and making them all wear a distinguishing mark in the form of a yellow star, herding them into "ghettoes" and then loading them into crowded cattle cars and dispatching them by train to concentration camps. There, they were either worked until they dropped, starved to death, or were gassed. All through the war, the long trains of Jewish prisoners rolled through Europe, taking their human cargo to be killed. Even at the end of the war, when Germany's defeat was obvious to everyone, the death trains continued to cross Europe, and the gas chambers continued to operate. Later, Jews were marched, or transported, from concentration camps outside Germany to other camps farther inland, many dying on these forced marches. The Nazis made sure that these Jews would be dead before the Allies could rescue them.

Both prior to the war and throughout the war years, the Nazis continuously depicted the Jews as "vermin" and as "sub-human." Their propaganda machine produced endless articles, caricatures, and films portraying Jews as greedy, grasping people who secretly "ruled the world," or as criminals who should be exterminated. It did not matter that the events of the war years proved decisively that the Jews were poor, weak, and powerless. In many countries of Europe, the inhabitants were rewarded for handing over Jews who had not yet been arrested. Here and there, however, some Europeans *did* risk their freedom, and even their lives, in order to help Jews and help conceal them from their Nazi oppressors. In Denmark, the king himself declared that he and the entire population would wear the yellow star, in sympathy with the Jews.

The Nazis used special terms, or euphemisms, to disguise their intentions and their treatment of the Jews. These constituted a "code," which sounded fairly harmless to those – including the victims – who were not fully aware of their real meaning. Thus, the cattle trucks and trains in which Jews were sent to the concentration camps were only "transports." Jews who had been designated for death in the camps underwent a "selection process," and the mass murders in the gas chambers constituted "special treatment." The total annihilation of the Jews of Europe was the "final solution of the Jewish problem."

Clearly, throughout World War II, from September 1939 until June 1945, Europe was ravaged by incessant war, its human and natural resources used by the German occupiers for their own ends, its cities bombarded and laid waste, and its population terrorized. By the time that the war had ended, millions of people had been killed or made homeless, exiled from their homes and separated from their families. Meanwhile, the systematic murder of six million Jews by the Nazis continued steadily and with brutal efficiency throughout all this chaos. When the war ended, the Jewish populations of Germany, Poland, Hungary, Czechoslovakia, Greece, Italy, France, Holland, Yugoslavia, and part of Russia, embodying a unique and age-old culture, had been virtually wiped out.

Despite the efforts which the Nazis made to keep their systematic murder of the entire Jewish and Gypsy populations of Europe secret, most people knew, at least in rumored theory, if not in detail, what fate awaited those Jews who were "sent East." The Nazis' brutality, their disregard for the sanctity of human life, as well as their efficiency and ingenuity, made it obvious to anyone of even moderate intelligence that the Jews were being sent to a bitter fate. Many people closed their eyes to the truth, refusing to admit even to themselves the full horror of what was happening, or perhaps unable to grasp to what depths human bestiality could descend, while others, such as the Franks' "protectors," did what they could to help Jews evade the Nazis. Anne writes in her diary that it was apparent to a number of "outsiders" – for example, the man who supplied their bread, as well as the greengrocer who provided their vegetables – that people were in hiding, but these Dutch people kept the group's secret, and even added extra rations when they could. Throughout Holland, some Jews, whether as individuals or as families, were kept in hiding in circumstances similar to those of the Frank family. There was a fairly active Dutch resistance movement, and this also played a part in ensuring that Jews were kept hidden and that their whereabouts did not become known to the Nazis. In every country which was occupied by the Nazis, a handful of that country's courageous individuals concealed Jews, and this happened even inside Germany itself, but the individuals who were capable of putting conscience above fear, prejudice, or envy were few and far between. In some cases, Jewish people managed to place children who looked "Aryan" – that is, those who were fair-haired and blue-eyed – in the homes of non-Jews who, whether for money or out of humanitarian considerations, sheltered them in their homes.

The Germans' euphemistic phrase, "the final solution of the Jewish problem," in fact, referred to the *total annihilation* of the Jewish population of Europe. Anne Frank's family, having moved to Holland from Germany in an attempt to escape Nazi persecution, and after living in hiding in the middle of Nazi-occupied Holland for two years, was discovered by the Nazis and sent to various concentration camps. All the members of the group in hiding, with the exception of Anne's father, Otto Frank, perished in those camps.

LIST OF CHARACTERS

The Group in Hiding

Anne Frank

The thirteen-year-old Jewish girl who writes a diary while she is hiding in Amsterdam from the Nazis during World War II.

Margot Frank

Anne's sister; she is three years older than Anne.

Otto Frank

Anne's father; he is a Jewish businessman who left Germany after Hitler's rise to power, hoping to find refuge in Holland.

Mrs. Frank

Anne's mother; she is the source of many conflicts with Anne during the two years that the family spends in hiding.

Mr. Van Daan

A Jewish businessman and an associate of Mr. Frank's. He and his family share the "Secret Annexe" with the Franks.

Mrs. Van Daan

Mr. Van Daan's wife; a rather interfering person. Anne finds it difficult to get along with her.

Peter Van Daan

The Van Daans' son; he is two-and-a-half years older than Anne, and his calm, quiet nature contrasts with her more excitable, vital personality. At first, Anne thinks that Peter is dull, but later on, they develop a warm and loving friendship.

Mr. Düssel

An elderly dentist who joins the group in hiding in November 1942. He shares Anne's room, and his pedantic nature continually irritates her.

The Dutch "Protectors" or "Helpers"

Mr. Kraler

A Dutch Gentile businessman who has been an associate of Mr. Frank and Mr. Van Daan and who takes over the running of the business when they are no longer able to do so. He works in the office in the building where the "Secret Annexe" is located, and he helps with technical, logistical aspects, such as obtaining food for the people in hiding.

Mr. Koophuis

A Dutch Gentile business associate of Mr. Frank and Mr. Van Daan. He also takes over the running of the business after all Jews have been forbidden to employ Gentiles, and he helps to conceal the group in hiding and obtain supplies for them.

Miep

A young woman who works in the office below the "Secret Annexe." She helps with obtaining food and supplies for the group in hiding and keeping their spirits up.

Elli

A young typist who also works in the office below the "Secret Annexe." She also helps obtain food and supplies for the group in hiding and comforts them psychologically.

CRITICAL COMMENTARIES

THE FIRST YEAR

June 1942–May 1943

Anne has just turned thirteen, and she lists the birthday presents which she has received, including the diary, which she says is "possibly the nicest of all." She then gives us a brief description of her personal history, mentioning her birth in Frankfurt, Germany, the family, their emigration to Holland after Hitler's rise to power and his persecution of the Jews in Germany, the Nazi occupation of Holland, among the Nazis' occupation of other European countries, plus the various, severe restrictions imposed upon Jews there. Anne describes all this in a very matter-of-fact way, listing the sorts of things that Jews must and must not do: "Jews must hand in their bicycles, Jews are banned from trains and are forbidden to drive. Jews are only allowed to do their shopping between three and five o'clock, and then only in shops which bear the placard 'Jewish Shop,'" and so on. She points out, however, that "life went on in spite of it all," and "things were still bearable" (June 20, 1942). Thus, in the midst of persecution and restrictions, Anne still describes her feelings about boyfriends and about girl friends, about school and her teachers, and also describes meeting Peter Wessel, a boy whom she apparently was rather fond of (June 30, 1942).

Anne's father tells her that at some future date the family will have to go into hiding in order to avoid being sent to concentration camps; to Anne, this all seems to be vaguely distant. Yet, suddenly, less than one month after the diary begins, the family does suddenly have to go into hiding because Anne's older sister, Margot, has been summoned by the Nazis to be sent to a concentration camp. All Jews knew that the concentration camps were terrible places of imprisonment, although the full extent of what was actually done there was not yet known. And so, the family had no choice; they packed a few basic possessions into shopping bags, put on as many items of clothing as they could, made arrangements for their cat to be looked after, and they set off on foot – in the rain – for the "hiding place" that Anne's father had been arranging and preparing for some time.

Straightaway, Anne and her father set about arranging and tidying the place, while Anne's mother and Margot lie down on their beds, too tired and emotionally drained and miserable to help (July 9–10, 1942).

The process of settling in and arranging a daily routine takes up several pages of the diary. At first, the Franks are alone, and the strange situation strikes Anne as "more like being on vacation in a very peculiar boardinghouse" than like being in hiding (July 11, 1942). Fear is an ever-present reality, however, as Anne writes, "It is the silence that frightens me so in the evenings and at night . . . I can't tell you how oppressive it is *never* to be able to go outdoors. Also, I'm very afraid that we shall be discovered and be shot" (July 11, 1942).

Anne then describes her surroundings and the considerable precautions which the family must take not to be seen or heard by anyone other than their "protectors"—namely, the workers in the office downstairs.

The second family, the Van Daans arrive, bringing new faces into the little group, but also new sources of irritation and conflict. Anne does not think very highly of young Peter Van Daan, who strikes her as being lazy, hypochondriacal, and boring. She is also shocked by the noisy quarrels between Mr. and Mrs. Van Daan, remarking rather self-righteously: "Mummy and Daddy would never dream of shouting at each other" (September 2, 1942).

Very perceptively, Anne describes the Van Daans' foibles and quirks. For example, Mrs. Van Daan is piqued that *her* dinner service—*and not the Franks'*—is put into communal use. Secretly, Anne knows, Mrs. Van Daan has removed three of her sheets from the collective linen cupboard. Mrs. Van Daan, who continually scolds Anne for her continuous chatter, also does her best to leave the washing up of the pots and pans for others to do (September 21, 1942). Mr. Van Daan tries to discipline Peter in a particularly overbearing way, but he is not very successful in this.

These may seem like small matters, but when people are confined within a small space, they get on one another's nerves so much more easily and for smaller causes. It is Anne's father who is always the "peacemaker" in the "Secret Annexe," the one who always has to assume the responsibility for "pouring oil on troubled waters" and soothing ruffled feelings.

In fact, Anne's father does his best to keep the younger members of the group busy, assigning them study tasks to do and ensuring that there is a constant supply of books for them to read as well. They all follow events in the outside world on a clandestine radio, and Anne struggles valiantly with French lessons. She also quarrels with her mother and complains to her diary that she cannot understand her mother and that her mother cannot understand her. Anne also resents the interference of the other members of the group. To illustrate this, Anne quotes a "squabble" with Mrs. Van Daan during dinner one night, ending with Mrs. Van Daan's saying to Anne's father, "I wouldn't put up with it if Anne were my daughter." According to Anne, these *always* seem to be Mrs. Van Daan's first and last words: "if Anne were my daughter." Understandably Anne confides to her diary, "Thank heavens I'm not!" (September 27, 1942).

Anne suffers a great deal from the constant criticism of the other members of the group in hiding; she is confused herself, and unable to understand fully the emotional suffering and horrible fears of both her own family and the Van Daans. In particular, though, Anne feels that her mother is not defending her sufficiently, and Anne resents the fact that she has *always* to keep so very quiet and restrain her adolescent impulse to "sass people back."

Anne also gives us a fairly detailed description of the washing and lavatory arrangements, which are far from ideal. Again, the stress in her relations with her family is not easy. Clearly, she feels a greater affinity with her father than with her mother, and it appears that there are various "scenes" and quarrels because of what her mother perceives as Anne's faults and failings. As always, Mr. Frank attempts to improve the situation and asks Anne to be more helpful in the house, but Anne stubbornly declines, preferring to concentrate her efforts on her schoolwork.

The war news filtering in from the outside is bad, and the little group in hiding hears that many of their Jewish friends have been taken away, crowded into cattle trucks and sent off to concentration camps, first in Holland, and then farther east, into Poland. Anne asks herself, "If it is as bad as this in Holland, whatever will it be like in the distant and barbarous regions they are sent to? We assume that most of them are murdered. The English radio speaks of their being gassed" (October 9, 1942).

An admirable attempt is made to celebrate the birthdays of the little group, and everyone tries to procure a little gift, through the people in the office, who constitute their only link with the outside world. Generally, these gifts consist of items of food, but also, they occasionally include such "luxuries" as flowers and books – things we take for granted, but which were precious for the little group in the "Secret Annexe."

Anne's relations with her family continue to fluctuate. On October 16, 1942, she writes, "Mummy, Margot, and I are as thick as thieves again. It's really much better," and then she describes how she and Margot squeezed together into bed, letting one another read parts of their diaries – and also, girl-like, discussing their "looks."

Then on November 7, Anne writes: "Mummy is frightfully irritable and that always seems to herald unpleasantness for me. Is it just a chance that Daddy and Mummy never rebuke Margot and that they always drop on me for everything?"

Clearly, the situation of being in hiding in the midst of a busy city produces many hours of extreme fear and tension – especially for an adolescent girl. When a workman comes to fill the fire extinguishers in the house, his noises terrify the unsuspecting, frightened little group, and they fear that their hiding place has been discovered. Anne writes: "My hand still shakes, although it's two hours since we had the shock" (October 20, 1942).

Anne further reveals the turmoil of her feelings about her family with startling frankness. "I'm not jealous of Margot, never have been. I don't envy her good looks or her beauty. It is only that I long for Daddy's real love: not only as his child, but for me – Anne, myself" (November 7, 1942). Anne feels again and again that her mother is unfair to her, and occasionally she feels that her mother is inadequate as a mother, yet Anne does try very hard not to pass too severe a judgment on her for this. Her remarks here, however, reveal a very perceptive and sensitive girl of thirteen: "Mummy and her failings are something I find harder to bear than anything else. I don't know how to keep it all to myself. . . . I have in my mind's eye an image of what a perfect mother and wife should be; and in her whom I must call "Mother" I find no trace of that image. . . . Sometimes I believe that God wants to try me, both now and later on; I must become good through my own efforts, without examples and without good advice. . . . From whom but myself shall I get comfort? As I need comforting often, I frequently feel weak, and dissatisfied with myself; my short-comings are too great. I know this, and every day I try to improve myself, again and again" (November 7, 1942).

Anne finds a great deal of solace in her diary; it is, in effect, her best friend, her confidante; she calls it "Kitty," and on its pages she feels absolutely free to complain of her sense of frustration at not being able to give vent to her feelings. But, most of all, she feels frustrated because she has no real person whom she can truly confide in – and receive encouragement from – just through expressing her feelings. Only her diary can do that for her.

Under normal circumstances, Anne would probably have confided her feelings to a friend, but these were *not* normal circumstances, and the only outlet for Anne's emotions lay within the pages of the small, red-checkered, cloth-covered diary.

In addition, Anne also gives factual accounts of some humorous events that occur, such as the splitting of a seam on a sack of beans which Peter was carrying up the stairs, so that "a positive hailstorm of brown beans came pouring down and rattled down the stairs . . . [I was] standing at the bottom of the stairs, like a little island in the middle of a sea of beans!" (November 9, 1942). She also recounts the serious discussion which precedes the decision as to whether or not they should take in an eighth person, an elderly dentist, Albert Düssel, who will have to move into Anne's room because of a lack of space.

Living in such cramped conditions with seven other people is bound to take its toll on anyone, particularly when discovery means almost certain death, yet Anne always tries to accept their situation in a positive way and to keep her spirits up: "Quite honestly, I'm not so keen that a stranger should use my things, but one must be prepared to make some sacrifices for a good cause, so I shall make my little offering with a good will. 'If we can save someone, then everything else is of secondary importance,' says Daddy, and he's absolutely right" (November 19, 1942).

That very evening, bad news from outside reaches the group in the "Secret Annexe," and Anne describes it vividly in her diary: "When it is dark, I often see rows of good, innocent people accompanied by crying children, walking on and on, in charge of a couple of these chaps, bullied and knocked about until they almost drop." Despite the difficulties and privations of living in hiding, however, Anne *realizes* that she is far more fortunate than a great many of her friends: ". . . who have now been delivered into the hands of the cruelest brutes that walk the earth. And all because they are Jews!" (November 19, 1942).

The Jewish festival of lights (Hannuka) occurs almost at the same time as the Dutch Festival of Saint Nicholas Day, and the members of the little group exchange gifts and light the traditional candles of the festival, although the group keeps them alight for only ten minutes because of the shortage of candles. Their "protectors" give them presents for the Dutch Festival of Saint Nicholas Day, attaching a little poem for each person and trying their best to lighten the tedium of their caged lives. And tedium it is – rarely, but occasionally, relieved. For instance, Anne describes the lengthy, prudent process whereby Mr. Van Daan prepares sausages, and then she tells in hilarious detail how the dentist, Mr. Düssel, examines the hysterically nervous Mrs. Van Daan's teeth, reminding Anne of "a picture from the Middle Ages entitled 'A Quack At Work'" (December 10, 1942). She also describes the scene which she can see in the street below the window and the joy of the group in hiding at receiving extra rations of butter for Christmas. To divert themselves, they all talk about what they will do "when the war is over" although they do not forget to feel sorry for the people outside who are taken away from their homes each day, or are unable to obtain enough food.

As the weeks grow into months, the little group in the "Secret Annexe" has, as might be expected, its ups and downs, quarreling with one another and incessantly criticizing its youngest member, the spirited Anne (who often cries at night because of the group's irritable remarks). The members of the group also talk about their respective childhoods and occasionally laugh at funny remarks made – whether intentionally or not – by one or another of their number. The fact that the building in which they are hiding and which serves as offices is being sold to a new owner (the offices were only leased from the former owner) gives the group some cause for alarm, but the problem is finally overcome.

And then more tedium sets in again, and as a diversion Anne and Margot are given card index boxes so that they can keep an account of the books they have read; Anne is also given a little notebook for foreign words she masters. Butter and margarine are distributed carefully and in rationed quantities to each person. At one point, Anne writes, "Lately Mummy and I have been getting on better together, but we still *never* confide in each other" (February 27, 1943). It is sometimes painful to read these intimate confessions.

On March 10, 1943, Anne mentions the bombing of Amsterdam by the planes of the Allies and the firing of the anti-aircraft guns, which disturb their sleep almost every night while they are in hiding. Although Anne knows that it is childish, she always creeps into her father's bed for comfort, unable to overcome her fears by herself.

The news from the outside world continues to raise – and then dash – the hopes of the group. On March 18, 1943, Anne writes excitedly that Turkey has entered the war, but the next day, it is announced that this is not, in fact, the case. Anne also describes a visit made by Hitler to wounded soldiers, a visit which is broadcast over the radio. She remarks, "Listening in to it was pitiful. . . . One of them [the wounded] felt so moved at being able to shake hands with the Führer (that is, if he still had a hand!) that he could hardly get the words out of his mouth" (March 19, 1943).

Because of the circumstances of being in strict hiding during the midst of the outside world's "ordinary life," every small noise or sudden suspicion of being discovered is a cause for serious alarm for the group. Although the men of the group try to be chivalrous and protect the women from becoming so anxious, it is not always possible. Since the group is in the habit of using the offices downstairs in order to listen to the radio there, or go to the bathroom after the office and warehouse staff have gone home, they are more exposed to being discovered than if they had remained in their hiding place, behind the false bookcase, all the time. Whether or not the alarms and fears of a burglary which they occasionally experience are genuine or imagined, real terror is struck into the hearts of everyone, causing them all to cower in dread, trying to keep quiet. Anne recounts the effect which this has on them all and how none of them can sleep afterward because they are so afraid (March 25, 1943).

After Anne confides to her diary, in a rather contemptuous way, about the real (or imagined) sickness of Mr. Van Daan, she changes the tone of her diary entry, giving the essence of a speech made by one of the German leaders in the Netherlands, declaring that the Nazis have decreed that a new objective within Holland will soon be "cleaning out" the various Dutch provinces of Jews. Anne notes that the terms which the "German big shots" use are reminiscent of those employed in getting rid of cockroaches, and then she revealingly remarks, "These wretched people are sent to filthy slaughterhouses like a herd of sick, neglected cattle. But I won't talk about it, I only get nightmares from such thoughts" (March 27, 1942).

Once again, the topic of Anne's relationship with her parents is discussed in her diary. She has unintentionally hurt her mother's feelings by refusing to say her prayers with her (because Anne's father cannot do so that night). Anne tries to reason with herself, feeling sorry for her mother, yet she refuses to apologize for saying what she considered to be the *truth* at the time about how she felt. Anne states quite clearly that her mother has alienated her with her "tactless remarks and crude jokes, which I don't find at all funny" (April 2, 1943). Later, that same month, Anne lists her quarrels with her mother as just one of the various clashes going on amongst *all* the members of the group, adding that "everyone is angry with everyone else" (April 27, 1943). At that time, the Allied air raids were increasing in intensity, and Anne writes, "We don't have a single quiet night. I've got dark rings under my eyes from lack of sleep." In addition, the shortage of food is beginning to be even more acute although in her following entry (May 1, 1943), Anne reminds herself: ". . . it is a paradise compared with how other Jews who are not in hiding must be living."

Nevertheless, despite her realization that their situation is better than that of many other Jews, Anne is horrified by the *drastic* decline of *their own* standards. The comfortable life which they had lived beforehand, and even, to some extent, in the "Secret Annexe" has declined rapidly. Their former life contrasts starkly with the privations which they are suffering now, ranging from a lack of food, to the inability to change their sheets, or even to renew their diminishing stock of underwear. The nightly air raids continue, and Anne prepares a suitcase with the basic things she would need if she had to escape, though she realizes, at her mother's prompting, that there would be nowhere for her to escape to – absolutely nowhere.

The last entry before Anne's fourteenth birthday contains news from the outside world relating to an air battle between German and British planes. The group also learns about strict new regulations concerning Dutch university students which have been imposed by the Nazis. Anne also mentions the fact that the group in the "Secret Annexe" must burn its vegetable peelings and refuse every other day, even though the weather is quite warm, because they must not put *anything* in the garbage pails for fear that even this might lead to their discovery. She remarks: "How easily one could be betrayed by being a little careless!" (May 18, 1943).

This innocent remark is bitterly ironic in view of the group's eventual fate.

The air raids continue to be as frightening as usual, but Anne and the others find relief in nervous laughter at the comical remarks of Mr. Düssel, especially when Mrs. Van Daan goes downstairs to Mr. Düssel's room, ". . . seeking there the rest which she could not find with her spouse," and Düssel receives her with the words, "Come into my bed, my child!"

Anne remarks, "This sent us off into uncontrollable laughter. The gunfire troubled us no longer, our fear was banished!" (May 18, 1943).

This first year of Anne's diary has been eventful, to put it mildly. From being a normal Dutch girl going to school and having fun with her friends, she has been forced to go into hiding and to be shut up with another seven individuals, unable to go outside, and live as other youngsters do. Apart from the problems which she experiences in her relations with her mother and her sister – problems which are fairly normal for any adolescent – she is also obliged to contend with the problems of being confined in a rather small area with a group of people who generally irritate and annoy her.

In addition to the difficulties of coping with her emotions and the changes in her body – another normal feature of adolescence – Anne has had to come to terms with the privations, the crowded and insanitary conditions and – most especially – with the ever-constant fear of being discovered and hauled away to one of the Nazi death camps.

The voice of the somewhat spoiled young girl who begins the diary changes by the end of this first year to the voice of a young girl who is able to analyze situations and characters, find amusement rather than annoyance in the little incidents of daily life, and put them all down on paper in a vivid, graphic way. She decidedly has a way with words, and her delicate irony, the way she records conversations, and her ability to describe scenes all enable *us* to experience and see and feel what she herself is undergoing.

THE SECOND YEAR

June 1943–August 1944

Anne's fourteenth birthday is celebrated with little gifts from the members of her "family in hiding," as she calls them, and she also receives a poem from her father. This was a German tradition, and as Anne's family had originally come from Germany, moving to Holland only after the rise to power of the Nazis in Germany, Anne's father wrote the poem in German. Margot, Anne's sister, translated it "brilliantly" into Dutch, and the English translator has also done a good job.

The Nazis have begun to move quickly; new regulations have been imposed. All civilians are ordered to hand in their radio sets (listening to stations other than those of the Nazis had been forbidden since the beginning of the war, but the Dutch people, nevertheless, listened to the BBC secretly, drawing encouragement from it), and the little group in the "Secret Annexe" is reluctantly obliged to forfeit the large set which was in the office downstairs. One of their "protectors," however, promises to provide them with another, substitute radio, and Anne concludes this entry by saying, "It is really true that as the news from the outside gets worse, so the radio with its miraculous voice helps us to keep up our morale and to say again, 'Chins up, stick it out, better times will come!'" (June 15, 1943).

Almost a month passes without an entry in Anne's diary, and then we read that Anne has decided to control her public remarks about the people whom she must be confined with, even if this involves shamming (or fraudulent behavior) ". . . so that the rain of rebukes dies down to a light summer drizzle" (July 11, 1943). Thus, the routine life of the group goes on, and Anne and Margot are even allowed to help a little with the work of the office downstairs, making them feel quite important. Anne mentions again how very important books are to her, as she is shut up in the "Secret Annexe" and has no other amusements.

She then describes – in a very detailed entry – how she approached her roommate, Mr. Düssel, very politely, after having first discussed the matter with her father. She asks Mr. Düssel if she may use the work table in their room for an extra hour-and-a-half twice a week. She explains that there is too much going on in the common room, and that although she is able to work on the table every day from half-past two until four, while Düssel sleeps, she needs more time to work. She is very disappointed and angry when Düssel absolutely refuses her request without giving any explanation. Yet, Anne keeps her temper and asks him to reconsider. She then recounts Düssel's selfish, melodramatic, and false tirade against her, again describing her own self-restraint and the immense mental effort that this discipline represents for her. Eventually, at her request, her father intervenes on Anne's behalf, and Düssel gives in. Anne concludes: "Düssel . . . didn't speak to me for two days and still had to go and sit at the table from five till half-past – frightfully childish. A person of fifty-four who is still pedantic and small-minded must be so by nature, and will never improve" (July 13, 1943).

Various events occur to alarm the group in the "Secret Annexe." The offices downstairs are burglarized, although this is noticed only after it has occurred sometime during the night (July 16, 1943). The air raids continue by day as well as by night, so that there is a constant fear of both fire and discovery. The news that Mussolini has resigned provides some encouragement, but the emotional and physical exhaustion resulting from the sleepless nights of the air raids continues (July 26, 1943).

In the following entry, Anne describes her efforts to find a neutral topic of conversation while she is doing the dishes with Mrs. Van Daan and Mr. Düssel, and how this tactic not only fails, but backfires because of a critical comment that Anne makes of a book which Düssel has recommended. This sets off Düssel and Mrs. Van Daan on a long tirade about how badly brought-up Anne is and how her ideas and opinions are *all wrong*. Anne comments perceptively: "I suppose it's their idea of a good upbringing to always try to set me against my parents, because that is what they often do" (July 29, 1943). Anne then allows herself to note all of her criticisms of Mrs. Van Daan, describing her as "very pushing, selfish, cunning, and calculating," but adds in a postscript: "Will the reader take into consideration that when this story was written the writer had not cooled down from her fury!"

Anne begins to give a detailed account of the group's daily routine, starting on August 4, 1943, with an account of their evening and night-time routines, who sleeps where, who washes when and how Anne leaves hairs in the bathroom sink. She also describes the strange noises which the house and its "inmates" make during the night. There is also a graphic description of Anne using the potty in the middle of the night, waking up from a dream to the sound of an air raid and scampering into her father's bed in fear. This last episode is illustrated by a verse from the poem which Margot wrote for Anne's birthday. Anne continues her account the following day with a description of lunchtime. Her review of the evening meal becomes an analysis of the characters of the people sitting around the table, their eating habits, their ways of talking, and their general traits. On the whole, these are not very complimentary.

In the passage for August 18, 1943, Anne manages to give a vivid and entertaining account of a rather mundane task, potato peeling. She has a keen eye, and she carefully observes the little nuances of speech and the physical gestures which characterize the various members of the group. There is also a touching description of what Anne calls "a little bit of real family life" (August 23, 1943).

The members of the group are up before half-past eight, when the workers begin their duties in the warehouse, and even though the office staff has not yet arrived, so that it is necessary for the group to be particularly quiet, Anne and Margot and their parents sit, read, or work in their room until it is time for breakfast, at nine o'clock.

The news about Italy's capitulation raises everyone's spirits (September 10, 1943), but this is offset by the illness of one of their "protectors," Mr. Koophuis. Another cause for concern is the fact that one of the workers in the warehouse appears to suspect something, and thus the already strained nerves of the members of the group lead them to virtually refrain from speaking to one another because "whatever is said you either annoy someone or it is misunderstood." Anne takes sedatives to calm her nerves (and so presumably do the others), but she notes that "it doesn't prevent me from being even more miserable the next day. A good hearty laugh would help more than ten Valerian pills, but we've almost forgotten how to laugh" (September 16, 1943). This remark, "but we've almost forgotten how to laugh," is but one of the many of Anne's comments that suggests that here is a person of a sensitivity, an intelligence, and a maturity far beyond her chronological years.

Mrs. Van Daan's birthday is celebrated, and the members of the group, as well as the "protectors," give her presents of things to eat, as well as some food coupons. Anne remarks: "Such are the times we live in!" (September 29, 1943). The strained relations between the members of the group continue, and Anne's words, "Oh, what kind of explosion is hanging over us now? If only I wasn't mixed up so much with all these rows! If I could only get away! They'll drive us crazy before long!" (September 29, 1943), are desperate cries from her heart.

One day, Mrs. Van Daan is obliged to sell her fur coat to raise money for food, and this leads to additional quarrels. Anne remarks, ironically: ". . . and now the reconciliation period of 'Oh, darling Putti' and 'precious Kerli' has set in." Then she adds: "I am dazed by all the abusive exchanges that have taken place in this virtuous house during the past month. . . . Quite honestly, I sometimes forget who we are quarreling with and with whom we've made it up. The only way to take one's mind off it all is to study, and I do a lot of that" (October 17, 1943).

Sundays – when there is no one working in the office, and when there is no relief from the tedium of the group – are particularly depressing days for Anne. She describes them with a telling phrase: "The atmosphere is so oppressive, and sleepy and as heavy as lead" (October 29, 1943). We can feel her painful desperation at being "jailed" for over a year when she writes: "I wander from one room to another, downstairs and up again, feeling like a songbird whose wings have been clipped and who is hurling himself in utter darkness against the bars of his cage" (October 29, 1943).

With an admirable sense of self-awareness, Anne writes, "If you were to read my pile of letters one after another, you would certainly be struck by the many different moods in which they are written. It annoys me that I am so dependent on the atmosphere here, but I'm certainly not the only one – we all find it the same" (November 8, 1943). She also gives us a very vivid account of her fears and nightmares, remarking that although she talks about the concept of "after the war," ". . . it is only a castle in the air, something that will never really happen." In this, she is being prophetic without even realizing it. Anne's diary entries now begin to show an increasing sense of sadness, desperation, and, occasionally, the loss of hope, although there is an entertaining interlude entitled "Ode to my Fountain Pen: In Memoriam," in which Anne recounts how she received her fountain pen as a gift from her grandmother when she was nine and how it was accidentally burned in the stove that day (November 11, 1943).

One night, Anne dreams about her best schoolfriend, Lies, and she is shot through with guilt at living in comfort and being unable to help Lies in any way. In her dream, Anne sees Lies "clothed in rags, her face thin and worn. Her eyes were very big" (November 27, 1943). This is an accurate description of the appearance of most of the concentration camp inmates, although Anne did not know – *and* could not have known – Lies' condition (sadly, ironically, Lies really was in a concentration camp).

The Dutch Festival of Saint Nicholas Day is celebrated with little poems which Anne and her father have written for everybody, and Christmas is marked by the exchange of small gifts. Anne has recovered from a bad bout of flu and comments that they "are all getting on well together for a change! There's no quarrelling – we haven't had such peace in the home for at least half a year" (December 22, 1943).

Anne's account of her feelings is extremely, almost achingly, honest in the entry for December 24, 1943, when she writes at length about her longing to go outside, to walk about freely, to do the things that young people all over the world do and, above all, to simply "have fun." This futile wish leads her once again to the sad topic of what she considers to be the inadequacies of her mother, and Anne vows to behave differently when she has children of her own. Anne seems to have expected too much of her mother, who would probably have functioned well enough in normal circumstances, but here – in this horrible situation – Mrs. Frank appears to be almost unable to understand her mercurial daughter, a girl of high intelligence and sensitivity. Remember that these are exceptional and dangerous conditions in which the Franks are trying to survive, and Mrs. Frank is just an ordinary, middle-class person with, perhaps, a limited imagination.

Anne mentions the fact that the mere act of writing her thoughts down in her diary has improved her mood a little. She also refers to her father's phrase "the love of his youth" (December 25, 1943), realizing that her father had confided in her concerning this person the previous year, but then she had not been able to understand "the meaning of his words" because he had to "express his own feelings for once" rather than coping with those of others. Anne adds that her father "has become very tolerant. I hope that I shall grow a bit like him, without having to go through all that [suffering]." This entry reveals Anne's sensitive awareness of her own faults and her desire to improve herself, as well as showing us Anne's acute consciousness of the feelings of others.

Anne's moods continue to swing back and forth between grief, compassion, and guilt. She grieves for the past and for loved ones who are gone, and there is also Anne's ever-growing compassion for those Jews whose suffering is greater than hers; in particular, she thinks about her girl friend Lies (December 29, 1943). She also feels guilty for having negative feelings about her mother (January 2, 1944). Anne seems to be becoming more aware of what it is that she believes that her mother lacks (January 5, 1944) – namely, a certain sensitivity to the feelings of her lively, moody adolescent daughter, and although this does not really ease Anne's pain at being misunderstood, it does help her to cope with it.

Anne's longing for a girl friend (January 5, 1944) is partly fulfilled when, on January 6, 1944, Anne decides to go up to Peter Van Daan's room and talk to him. Peter is a rather shy boy, two years older than Anne, and it seems that he is not averse to having Anne come and talk to him. Anne, however, is torn between her need for someone to confide in and her fear of seeming to be "too forward," but she concludes, "Don't think I'm in love with Peter – not a bit of it! If the Van Daans had had a daughter instead of a son, I should have tried to make friends with her too."

That night, Anne dreams about a former boyfriend, also called Peter, dreaming about him in a rather romantic way, and she feels certain, upon waking, that "Peter was still the chosen one." This leads her, in her next diary entry, on January 7, 1944, to relate the history of all her boyfriends at the various stages of her life. We realize here that her relationship with Peter Van Daan compensates for many of the difficulties of her daily life, for Anne writes, "What do I care about the lot of them! Peter belongs to me and no one knows anything about it. This way I can get over all the snubs I receive. Who would ever think that so much can go on in the soul of a young girl?" (January 12, 1944).

After writing rather antagonistically about the faults of the Van Daans, Anne comes to realize that the faults which she sees in them might not necessarily be theirs alone. It is a very perceptive and mature Anne who writes, "Until now I was immovable! I always thought the Van Daans were in the wrong, but we too are partly to blame. We have certainly been right over the subject matter; but handling of others from intelligent people (which we consider ourselves to be!) one expects more insight. I hope that I have acquired a bit of insight and will use it well when the occasion arises" (January 22, 1944).

Another milestone of maturity is passed when Anne manages to have a conversation with Peter about sex, when he shows her his cat's male organs. Anne feels strange, but she admires Peter for being able to talk about it in a matter-of-fact way. Other than that, the normal daily routines of the little group continue. Anne is still involved in her studies, but she also occupies herself with compiling the family trees of the royal families of Holland and England, as well as collecting pictures of the various movie stars of the time. The adults continue to annoy her by repeatedly telling the same anecdotes, and, in a telling phrase, she marvels at the fact that "we are quite as used to the idea of going into hiding, or 'underground,' as in bygone days one was used to Daddy's bedroom slippers warming in front of the fire" (January 28, 1944). Their "protectors" continue to help and encourage them, even though this involves danger for them, and Anne regards this as being on a par with all other acts of heroism performed during the war, vowing never to forget them.

The probability of an invasion of Europe by the Allies (the forces fighting against the Nazis) increases, and all sorts of rumors and speculations are talked about and considered. The group in the "Secret Annexe" is aware of all this through their "protectors," as well as through listening to the BBC. Anne gives examples of the kinds of conversations conducted by the members of the group, concluding rather fatalistically, "I myself keep very quiet and don't take any notice of all the fuss and excitement. I have now reached the stage that I don't care much whether I live or die. The world will still keep on turning without me; what is going to happen, will happen, and anyway it's no good to resist. I trust to luck and do nothing but work, hoping that all will end well" (February 3, 1944).

Anne's growing relationship with Peter continues to excite and console her, even though she remains terribly frustrated by having to remain inside – especially now, when spring is beginning, filling her with longings "to talk, for freedom, for friends, to be alone!" (February 12, 1944). Peter confides in her about his frustration at being unable to express himself clearly, as he claims she does, and even though she feels that this is not justified, and that she is equally tongue-tied or unnecessarily verbose, she feels glad "because I sensed a real feeling of fellowship, such as I can only remember having had with my girlfriends" (February 14, 1944). On another occasion, Peter helps Anne find the smallest and sweetest potatoes, and Anne feels that he is looking at her with "such a gentle warm look which made a tender glow within me. I could really see that he wanted to please me, and because he couldn't make a long complimentary speech he spoke with his eyes" (February 16, 1944).

Although Anne now feels much happier and is always hoping to see "him" when she goes upstairs, she still experiences sudden moods of unhappiness, when the tears simply roll down her cheeks, and she feels uncertain of Peter's affection for her (February 19, 1944). Anne does find some solace, though, in going up to the attic, where Peter works, and from where she can look up through the skylight at "the bare chestnut tree, on whose branches little raindrops shine, appearing like silver, and at the seagulls and the other birds as they glide on the wind" (February 23, 1944). From that room, Anne can also look out over Amsterdam, gaze at the roofs, and at the horizon, and in her misery, she finds that this communion with nature, and with the things that seem *more permanent than man,* bring peace to her soul.

As her concern with Peter increases steadily, so that she "hardly does anything else but think of Peter" (February 27, 1944), Anne realizes that there are a great many similarities between them. Both of them, she feels, have mothers who are inadequate, and both she and Peter wrestle continually with their inner emotions. She notes, however, that whereas *her* reaction is to be noisy and boisterous, Peter is more likely to sink into silence. In a sad mood, Anne ends this entry for February 28, 1944, with the plaintive cry, "I'm sentimental—I know. I'm desperate and silly—I know that too. Oh, help me!"

A burglary in the office downstairs alarms the members of the little group again, although fear does *not* seem to play such a large part in their lives as it did at the beginning of their period of hiding. Anne, *in particular,* appears to be less fearful about things than she was before, possibly because she has developed a more fatalistic attitude, as her entry for February 3, 1944, shows. Still, though, she continues to resent the fact that grownups treat her, Margot, and Peter as "children" and prevent them from expressing their opinions about such subjects as overcoming depression and feelings of discouragement, which they feel as well-equipped as the adults to discuss.

Anne finally admits to herself that her feelings for Peter are "pretty near to being in love with him" (March 3, 1944), and each entry in her diary records another topic of conversation discussed or another meeting between them. Anne realizes that Peter is very shy, and she does not want to appear too eager herself, so both of them seem to be hovering on the brink of declaring their love. She writes, "Who will be the first to discover and break through this armor?" And she then adds, "I'm glad after all that the Van Daans have a son and not a daughter; my conquest could never have been so difficult, so beautiful, so good, if I had not happened to hit on someone of the opposite sex" (March 6, 1944).

In one of her more introspective moods, Anne looks back to the girl she was and to the life which she led before she went into hiding, noting that ". . . it all seems so unreal. It was quite a different Anne who enjoyed that heavenly existence from the Anne who has grown wise within these walls" (March 7, 1944). While recognizing that her life beforehand had been enjoyable, she admits that she was certainly more superficial then, and that she will never again be able to live like that, at least not for long stretches of time. She maintains that even then she felt a certain emptiness, but disguised it with a constant flurry of activities and friends. She also analyzes the various phases which she has gone through after going into hiding. She speaks of her initial confusion, followed by depression and then, as she began to mature, both physically and emotionally, she describes her growing self-awareness, and finally, her discovery of her inward happiness through her close relationship with Peter Van Daan.

The daily problems of obtaining and preparing food, getting along with the various members of the group, contacts with the outside world and news of the progress of the war still occupy Anne's thoughts to a considerable extent. But some things have changed. Anne's feelings about Peter, for example, cause her to be very reserved with her family, and she says, ". . . the brightest spot of all is that at least I can write down my thoughts and feelings, otherwise I would be absolutely stifled!" (March 16, 1944).

As we read, we realize that Anne continues to resent being cooped up with the other members of the group and that she still objects to being treated as a child, for she says, "Although I'm only fourteen, I know quite well what I want, I know who is right and who is wrong, I have my opinions, my own ideas and principles, and although it may sound pretty mad from an adolescent, I feel more of a person than a child, I feel quite independent of anyone" (March 17, 1944).

More and more, Peter and Anne confide in one another, and Anne records their conversations in her diary. As they open their hearts to one another, talking about their initial impressions of one another when the group first went into hiding, they realize that they have even more in common than they had ever imagined. Anne, however, is sad at the thought that Margot is made wretched by Anne's relationship with Peter, since Margot also likes him, but Margot assures Anne, in a letter, that it is not that *she herself* loves Peter, but, rather, that she regrets not having found anyone for herself yet. This sets off a touching exchange of letters between Margot and Anne, in which each one shows her concern for the other's feelings. It was obviously easier for them both to set their emotions down on paper than to talk about them face-to-face.

Both Anne and Peter have to take a fair amount of teasing from the adults about the fact that Anne goes up to Peter's room in the evenings, and Anne remarks that "we don't take much notice of all this parental chatter, their remarks are so feeble. Have the two sets of parents forgotten their own youth? It seems like it, at least they seem to take us seriously, if we make a joke, and laugh at us when we are serious" (March 23, 1944). In this, she is probably speaking for a great many teenagers who have often felt misunderstood and mistreated by their parents.

Although Anne states quite clearly that politics do *not* interest her, she nevertheless describes the reactions of the various members of the group to the news which they hear over the radio or from their "protectors." For example, she depicts one scene as they all sit around the radio, listening to a speech given by Winston Churchill; yet, following the speech, the heated arguments that ensue horrify and anger her (March 27, 1944).

Anne continues to be more preoccupied with Peter and with the growing closeness between them. She also continues to resent her mother's interference, although she admires her father's restraint at his daughter's obvious interest in Peter.

One day, one of the BBC broadcasts contains a suggestion by one of the Dutch leaders in exile that after the war the diaries and letters of people who have been through the war should be published. This causes quite a stir among the members of the group in hiding, and Anne starts to entertain serious thoughts of publishing her diary at a later stage, remarking that "it would seem quite funny ten years after the war if we Jews were to tell how we lived and what we ate and talked about here" (March 29, 1944). This sentence is strangely prophetic, as Anne's diary is, indeed, one of the most vivid documents—and perhaps the best-known—that has survived from that period, giving us a painfully honest, human "inside view" of what it was like to be Jewish and to be hiding in perpetual fear during the war years.

Time and time again, Anne wrestles with depression, struggling to hold back tears when she is with Peter, bravely endeavoring not to sob out loud when she is alone. She tries to reason with herself, and eventually she succeeds, writing, "It was over!" (April 4, 1944). On the same occasion, she gives us a far more hopeful and more positive account of what she wants her future to be, so that the gloomy entry which began – "For a long time I haven't had any idea of what I was working for any more; the end of the war is so terribly far away, so unreal, like a fairy tale" – becomes more optimistic: "I must work, so as not to be a fool, to get on, to become a journalist, because that's what I want! I know that I can write."

This same entry reveals Anne becoming a more mature young woman, one who is able to appraise herself and her surroundings clearly and also critically. She knows that *she* is the best judge of her own work, and she also realizes that she wants more from life than being just a homemaker, as her mother is, and as the women of her class generally were. Here, too, Anne exhibits an awareness of the position of women, an attitude which is *far ahead of her time* and her immediate environment.

Anne also expresses her desire to go on living after her death, and she thanks God for her ability to write, declaring that it is writing that consoles and encourages her. How ironic it is to read Anne's heart-searching entries and her assertions about the future when we know, as she could not, that these hopes of hers were indeed fulfilled, but not in the way she expected, and that *the very words* which she was writing at that moment were to bring her far greater immortality than she could ever have imagined.

Another attempt by burglars to break into the warehouse downstairs forces the members of the group to cower almost motionless for hours, afraid that they have finally been discovered. Anne gives us a graphic description of their whispered conversation and the various sights, sounds, and smells of these long hours. The incident causes Anne to wonder at their fates as Jews; again, she states her belief that the suffering which they are undergoing is so that they may emerge stronger. She also affirms her love for the Dutch nation, its people and its language, asserting that she intends to remain in Holland after the war (April 11, 1944).

Anne is, figuratively, "up in the clouds" when Peter kisses her for the first time (April 16, 1944), although her doubts regarding the propriety of this, and the probable reactions of her parents and sister if they had known about it strike us as rather odd in this age of permissiveness. Although Peter and Anne would put their arms around one another, and, later on, occasionally kiss, their physical relationship was very innocent, a far different situation from the behavior of many teenagers today. In the space of only a few years, and with the help of medical advances in methods of birth control, sexual morality has changed tremendously. Once again, Anne displays astonishing maturity for a girl of fourteen by refusing to accept completely the extremely strict moral standards of her time, writing, ". . . we are shut up here, shut away from the world, in fear and anxiety, especially just lately. Why, then, should we who love each other remain apart? Why should we wait until we've reached a suitable age? Why should we bother?" (April 17, 1944).

Anne's happiness with Peter is not overshadowed by the daily trials of life in the "Secret Annexe." But perhaps Anne's awareness of what maturity means has been heightened, for it is a very perceptive, if disenchanted, Anne who writes that the ordinary man in the street is as much to blame for the war as are the politicians, and that there is a destructive urge in everyone, so that unless this changes, bloodshed will always continue. Nevertheless, her *irrepressible optimism* causes her to write: "I am young and I possess many buried qualities; I am young and strong and am living a great adventure; I am still in the midst of it and can't grumble the whole day long. I have been given a lot, a happy nature, a great deal of cheerfulness and strength. Every day I feel that I am developing inwardly, that the liberation is drawing nearer and how beautiful nature is, how good the people are about me, how interesting this adventure is! Why, then, should I be in despair?" (May 3, 1944).

Following the advice that Margot has given her, Anne writes a letter to her father, explaining her feelings about him and her mother, the difficulties she has been through during the period they have been in hiding and speaking honestly of her refusal to knuckle under to what she knows has been his silent disapproval of her relationship with Peter (May 5, 1944). Anne's father has a long and emotional talk

with her after this letter, and Anne regrets having wounded his feelings, acknowledging that she might have misjudged him.

Various setbacks – such as the arrest of the man who brought them
vegetables, rumors that there is growing anti-Semitism among the
Dutch people, and Anne's fears that, having been born in Germany,
she and her family will not be able to remain in Holland once the
war is over – cause Anne's spirits to fall. She wonders if they might
not all be better off dead, but still she clings to her hope that *something
will happen,* and that the war will end soon (May 26, 1944). The news
of the Allied invasion of Europe revives the optimism of the group,
and Anne's fifteenth birthday is celebrated in a spirit of greater cheerfulness (June 13, 1944).

The last few entries in Anne's diary are concerned with the various
daily events that Anne has written about all along – the moods of the
members of the group, their preoccupation with food, the books they
read and discuss, Anne's relations with her parents, and her feelings
toward Peter.

Anne's last entry, on August 1, 1944, three days before the "Secret
Annexe" is raided by the police and its occupants are sent to concentration camps, is one in which Anne analyzes herself and her situation, displaying considerable powers of perception. She concludes,
after acknowledging that her flippant behavior is just a front to help
her cope with the people around her, with the statement that she
keeps on "trying to find a way of becoming what I would so like to
be, and what I could be, if . . . there weren't any other people living
in the world."

At the end of the period of hiding, Anne is clearly a very different
person from the girl who started out to write in the red-checkered
diary; especially during the second year, she has matured greatly. Of
course, there has been the growing love between her and Peter, and
this has certainly left its mark. But in addition to the self-confidence
she has acquired, Anne is less quick to judge the other people around
her; she has a greater self-awareness now, and she has thought deeply
about a great many subjects.

Anne has not wasted her time while she has been in hiding. Under
her father's guidance, she has continued studying various subjects,
skills, and languages. She has developed her writing, especially, so
that the style in her diary has become more varied and vivid. In fact,
her diary contains descriptive passages, conversations, character

analyses, and honest introspection that we would not expect from such a young girl; this is one of the reasons why it has managed to capture the interest of so many people over such a long period of time; very simply, it is well-written. Anne's ability to analyze people and situations has grown as we watch, so to speak, so that we do not feel that we are reading the maudlin confessions of a "mixed-up" teenager; rather, we are eager to find out what this intelligent young woman has to say about the varied subjects which she chooses to write about. Being forced to remain in hiding for two years is obviously too high a price to pay for precocious maturity, but how much poorer our world would have been had we not been granted this glimpse into the inner workings of a young girl's mind in the years that were so fateful for her and for the whole world.

EPILOGUE

Of the eight people hiding in the "Secret Annexe," only one, Anne's father, survived. All their Dutch "protectors," or helpers, managed to live through the war, and even Anne's schoolfriend, Lies, about whom she thought and dreamed, and whom she mentions in the *Diary,* survived. In his book *Anne Frank: A Portrait in Courage,* Ernst Schnabel has retraced Anne's life. It starts in the town of Frankfurt, in the house where Anne spent her early childhood; Schnabel interviewed people who knew the Frank family in Frankfurt and, later, those who knew them in Amsterdam.

After the group's capture by the Nazis, they were taken back to Germany and were sent to concentration camps. Ernst Schnabel also interviewed people who had been in the camps with the Franks and had witnessed their final moments, as well as those of the other members of the group in hiding. In the following pages, you will find brief accounts of the backgrounds and fates of the characters in the poignant human drama revealed to us through Anne Frank's *The Diary of a Young Girl.*

CHARACTER BACKGROUNDS AND FATES

Anne Frank

Anne was born on June 12, 1929, three years after her sister,

Margot, in the town of Frankfurt-on-Main in Germany. Four years later, in the summer of 1933, the Frank family moved to Holland because Hitler had come to power in Germany and had introduced strict laws which discriminated against Jews. In addition, gangs of Nazi thugs would roam the streets, beating up Jews for no reason – except that they were Jews.

Anne attended the Montessori kindergarten and grade school in Amsterdam after the Germans invaded Holland in May, 1940, but the anti-Semitic regime from which the Frank family had sought to escape in Germany caught up with them. Anne and Margot, along with thousands of other Jewish children, were no longer allowed to attend schools of their own choosing and were obliged to go to only Jewish schools. Anne herself did not mind this, readily adapting to the new environment, making new friends and finding old ones among her classmates.

Realizing how dangerous the political situation was becoming, Mr. Frank prepared a refuge where his family could go into hiding, rather than submitting to arrest by the Nazis and being dispatched to concentration camps and to almost certain death. At the beginning of July, 1942, when it would have been foolish to delay not going into hiding, the Franks, and then a few days later, a family called the Van Daans, moved into the "Secret Annexe" in the building where Mr. Frank's offices and warehouse were situated; overnight, they simply vanished from sight.

As a child, Anne was bright and lively, not considered by her parents and their friends to be as intelligent and as beautiful as her sister, Margot, but nonetheless loved for her humor and personality. Anne does *not* conceal her awareness of this attitude in her diary, and her resentment of it perhaps adds to the irony that it should be Anne's name, rather than Margot's, that has become known to posterity. Perhaps this early, slight adversity strengthened in Anne a resolve to shine in some way and to prove to her family and to the world that she was not *just* the younger sister of the beautiful and talented Margot Frank.

As anyone who has read Anne's diary knows, she was immensely gifted, both as a writer and as a person of great sensitivity. She could feel things deeply, sense the feelings of others and communicate all this to paper. Anne's personality sparkles and shines on every page of the diary – whether Anne is in the heights of ecstasy over her budding relationship with Peter Van Daan or whether she is in the depths of despair over the grim realities of her life in hiding; whether she is describing the constant irritation of being confined to the house and having to live at such close quarters with people whom she dislikes, or whether she is confessing her ambivalent feelings toward her parents and her sister.

Above all else, Anne's feelings are ordinary and so akin to those experienced by any teenager growing up and being confronted by situations and with individuals which he or she is not yet capable of dealing with in a detached or adult way. One of the most striking features that emerges from Anne's diary is the sense of the *intensity* of the emotions that she experiences as an adolescent.

On August 4, 1944, the Gestapo, apparently acting on information provided by an informer, probably one of the workers in the warehouse, arrived at the building where the Franks were hiding, entered the office and began to search the building. Although Mr. Kraler tried to convince them that there was nothing behind the bookcase at the end of the corridor, the Nazis pulled it away, and the secret door to the Franks' hiding place was exposed.

No one acted hysterically or violently when they realized what had happened; in numbed silence, they simply put together a few basic possessions which they thought they might need and left with their captors. The notebooks in which Anne had written her diary were scattered on the floor and left there when one of the Gestapo men emptied a briefcase in an attempt to find money or any other "valuables." Another instance of the irony of fate.

The members of the Jewish group in hiding, together with Mr. Kraler and Mr. Koophuis, were taken to Gestapo headquarters in Amsterdam and locked in a room with other people who had been arrested. Later in the day, the Jewish prisoners were separated from the rest, and after being kept at headquarters for a few days for questioning, they were taken to the railroad station and transported to the Westerbork reception camp. They rode in a regular passenger train, and, according to the evidence of Mr. Frank, they were relatively cheerful. *They were together.* Moreover, they knew where they were going, although they did not know if they would be permitted to remain there for long, and they were aware that there was the possibility of deportation to Poland and the concentration camps there. But they also knew that the Allies were advancing, and they hoped that luck and faith would keep them out of the death camps until the war was over.

Throughout the journey, Mr. Frank relates, Anne remained glued to the window, seemingly absorbing as much as she could of the scenery of the summer countryside. Remember: Anne had not been outside for two whole years.

When the group arrived at Westerbork, they were made to stand in a long row in the mustering square while one of the clerks entered their names on a list. The conditions were bad, but not unbearable. Westerbork, after all, was merely a reception camp, and although there was overcrowding, deprivation, and undernourishment, there were no gas chambers or crematoriums, as there were at the concentration camps.

An eyewitness who was at Westerbork says, "I saw Anne Frank and Peter Van Daan every day in Westerbork. They were always together, and I often said to my husband: 'Look at those two beautiful young people.' . . . In Westerbork, Anne was lovely, so radiant that her beauty flowed over into Peter. She was very pallid at first, but there was something so intensely attractive about her frailty and her expressive face."

Seemingly, Anne was happy at Westerbork, despite everything. She could see new people and talk to them, after having been cooped up with the same seven people for over two years. The thought that occupied her mind most of all was whether they would be sent to Poland and whether or not they could live through the trying days ahead. Anne's father would visit her in the women's barracks sometimes in the evenings, standing by her bed and telling her stories. Similarly, when a twelve-year-old boy who lived in the women's barracks fell ill, Anne stood by his bed and talked to him in the same way.

On September 2, Anne, together with the other members of the group in hiding, was gathered into a group of one thousand persons and sent to Germany. They traveled in sealed railway cattle cars, seventy-five people crowded in each car, with only one, small, barred window, high up. The journey took several days, and on the third night, the train suddenly came to a stop. The doors of the car were jerked open, and blazing searchlights, SS men with dogs, and the bustling Kapos (prisoner-guards) constituted the prisoners' first glimpse of the Auschwitz concentration camp. As the passengers streamed out of the train, the men were ordered to go right, and the women were ordered to go to the left. Children and sick people were told to enter trucks painted with big red crosses to spare them the hour's march to the camp, but the trucks never arrived. The children and sick people who entered them were *never seen again.*

Anne, her mother, Margot, and Mrs. Van Daan all marched with the rest of the women to the camp, hustled along at a brutal pace by the SS guards and the Kapos. On arrival at the camp, everyone's head was shaved; yet a woman who was with Anne at that time said of Anne; "You could see that her beauty was wholly in her eyes. . . . Her gaiety had vanished, but she was still lively and sweet, and with her charm she sometimes secured things that the rest of us had long since given up hoping for.

"For example, we had no clothing aside from a gray sack, and under that we were naked. But when the weather turned cold, Anne came into the barracks one day wearing a suit of men's long underwear. She had begged it somewhere. She looked screamingly funny with those long white legs, but somehow still charming.

"We were divided into groups of five for roll call, work, and distribution of food. You see, we had only one cup to each group of five. Anne was the youngest in her group, but nevertheless she was the leader of it. She also distributed the bread in the barracks, and she did it so well and fairly that there was none of the usual grumbling."

With the sensitivity which she reveals in her diary, Anne must have suffered greatly, having to witness the daily acts of cruelty and suffering in the concentration camp. Many prisoners became immune to the torment of those around them, but Anne retained her sense of compassion, and she could still shed tears of pity and perform acts of kindness for others.

On October 30, 1944, there was a "selection," and all the women had to wait naked on the mustering ground for a long time, then march in single file into the barracks, where each one had to step into the bright beam cast by a cold searchlight. The infamous Dr. Mengele ordered those prisoners who were not too sick or too old to step to one side, and it was obvious to everyone that the others would be gassed. Anne and Margot passed the exam; they were deemed fit enough to be sent to the Belsen concentration camp, while their mother was not.

Once again, the prisoners were crowded into sealed cattle cars and sent on a long journey which lasted for several days. The train stopped and started, sometimes waiting for an hour at a time. Many passengers died of hunger or disease along the way.

When the train arrived in Belsen, SS guards were waiting on the platform with fixed bayonets. The prisoners were told to leave the dead lying in the cars and to line up in marching order. In the words of someone who was there at the same time as Anne, Belsen was different from Auschitz. "There was no regular work, as there had been at Auschwitz, although the prisoners were given the task of removing the dead, dragging them over the ground to the cremation area. There were no roll calls, nothing but people as fluttery from starvation as a flock of chickens, and there was neither food nor water nor hope, for it no longer meant anything to us that the Allies had reached the Rhine. We had typhus in the camp, and it was said that before the Allies came, the SS would blow us all up."

It was at Belsen that Anne and her schoolfriend, Lies, met again, for Lies and her family had been sent there earlier and had been placed in a separate section for "neutral foreigners." In that "privileged position," Lies was still able to receive packages through the Red Cross Organization. When she heard that a group of people had arrived from Auschwitz, Lies managed to make contact with Anne, across the barbed wire fence that separated them, and Lies describes her thus: "She was in rags. I saw her emaciated, sunken face in the darkness. Her eyes were very large. We cried and cried."

Anne was freezing and starving, and Lies attempted to get some extra food across the fence to her friend. She packed up a woolen jacket, zwieback (rusks), sugar, a tin of sardines, and threw it all across the fence. All she heard, however, were screams, and Anne crying. When she shouted and asked what had happened, Anne called back, weeping: "A woman caught it and won't give it to me." Lies told Anne to come back again the following night, and that time, Anne caught the packet, but this time it contained only zwieback and a pair of stockings.

Anne's sister, Margot, died of typhus at the end of February (or the beginning of March), after having been critically ill and in a coma for days. Anne was already sick at the time, and she was not informed about her sister's death. After a few days, however, Anne sensed what had happened, and soon afterward, she herself died, peacefully, feeling that nothing bad was happening to her, shortly before the camp was liberated by the Allies.

In summary, when the Nazis occupied Holland in 1940, Anne was only eleven years old. Like many parents, Mr. and Mrs. Frank tried to protect their children from the edicts issued by the Nazis, and although the girls knew that they had to change schools and wear the "yellow star" (signifying that they were Jews) on their clothes, they did not have any direct contact with Nazis. In general, the Dutch people were sympathetic to the plight of the Jews, and many of them helped them with a kind word or little gifts. The grisly, wholesale murder of Jews in concentration camps did not really get underway until 1942, and in 1940 no one could imagine that the annihilation of an entire people was possible.

By the time Anne and the others went into hiding, in June 1942, they knew that Jews were rounded up, beaten, stripped of their possessions, and sent East. They suspected that the conditions out there were not good, but Nazi propaganda insisted that the "resettlement" was to the Jews' benefit, and there was no clear information to be obtained as to what really went on there. In her diary, Anne writes: "Our many Jewish friends are being taken away by the dozen. These people are treated by the Gestapo without a shred of decency, being loaded into cattle trucks and sent to Westerbork. . . . Most of the people in the camp are branded as inmates by their shaven heads. . . . If it is as bad as this in Holland, whatever will it be like in the distant and barbarous regions they are sent to? We assume that most of them are murdered. The English radio speaks of their being gassed" (October 9, 1942).

From this, and other remarks which Anne makes, we know that she and the other members of the group in hiding knew what was happening to the Jews on the outside, to a greater or lesser extent. There was a radio in the office, and they would creep downstairs at night and listen to the BBC broadcasts, so that they had a fairly good idea of what was going on.

The windows of the "Secret Annexe" allowed its inmates to see something of what was going on in the streets outside, and on December 13, 1942, Anne writes, "I saw two Jews through the curtain yesterday; it was a horrible feeling, just as if I'd betrayed them and was now watching them in their misery." The members of the group of "protectors" (or helpers) also brought eyewitness accounts of what was happening to Jews outside.

Every sudden, unexplained noise, every real or imagined break-in by burglars, and every stranger who visited the office and the warehouse was a continuous source of fear and concern for the people in the "Secret Annexe." There were several occasions when they sat up all night, afraid to make a sound, fearing that they had heard someone moving around downstairs.

The Allies' air raids on Amsterdam, the anti-air cannon fired by the Nazis, and the aerial dog-fights between Nazi and Allied aircraft in the sky also constituted a source of alarm for the group in hiding. The building was old and could easily catch fire. For that reason, they had each prepared a small bag of basic necessities to grab in case they had to leave the building in a hurry. But that, of course, was the greatest danger, as it involved their worst fear of all: discovery by the Nazis.

"We had a short circuit last evening, and on top of that the guns kept banging away all the time. I still haven't got over my fear of everything connected with shooting and planes, and I creep into Daddy's bed nearly every night for comfort." That is how Anne's entry for March 10, 1943, begins. This kind of remark recurs at intervals through the diary, but it would seem that eventually the inmates of the "Secret Annexe" *did* become accustomed to the situation. After all, two years in hiding is *a long time,* and they knew that the Allies were advancing and the situation of the Nazis was deteriorating. By the time the diary ends, in August 1944, Anne had every reason to be optimistic, and she was even thinking about going back to school.

By the time they were arrested, the occupants of the "Secret Annexe" no longer seriously thought that they would be discovered. Although they had been frightened at the beginning, they had become used to their situation and hoped to continue in that way until the war ended. The news from the various war fronts was very good, and it was obvious that the Nazis *would* be defeated. If the discovery had only come a little later, if the group had not been included in the last shipment of people to leave Westerbork, if Anne had not been sent first to Auschwitz, and then to Belsen, who knows what might have happened?

When Anne's father returned to Amsterdam after the war had ended, Miep and Elli (the young workers in the office where the "Secret Annexe" was located) gave him the notebooks and papers in Anne's handwriting which they had found strewn over the floor of the "Secret Annexe" after the Gestapo police had left. At first, Otto

Frank had copies of the diary circulated privately, as a memorial to his family, but he was finally persuaded by a Dutch professor to publish it. After the *Diary's* initial appearance in Dutch in 1947, it quickly went through several editions and was translated into dozens of languages. The *Diary* was dramatized, and the play was presented on Broadway, winning the Pulitzer, Critics Circle, and Antoinette Perry Prizes for 1956. It has been made into a movie and has been adapted for television. The Anne Frank Foundation, founded by Otto Frank, maintains the building on the Prinsengracht Canal where the Franks hid for twenty-five months as a museum and memorial to Anne Frank. Each year, the house is visited by thousands of people from all over the world. The Foundation is trying to promote better understanding between young people from every part of the world, and it has established the International Youth Center, which serves as a meeting place for young people and holds lectures, discussions, and conferences covering a wide range of international problems.

The Montessori School in Amsterdam is now renamed the Anne Frank School, and there are other memorials to her in Germany, Israel, and elsewhere. But, above all, it is Anne's *Diary*, in which her unique, yet representative, voice is preserved, that constitutes the most eloquent memorial of all.

Margot Frank

Margot was three years older than Anne, so was probably more aware of the family's move from Germany to Holland, which took place when she was seven years old. Margot was a quiet, obedient child, who always kept her clothes neat and clean, unlike her younger sister. She was considered the more beautiful and the more intelligent of the two, and Anne resented her for this sometimes, as she notes in her diary.

Margot did well at school and was often used as an example for Anne by the Franks, who wanted Anne to copy Margot's good behavior. During the two years that they were confined in the "Secret Annexe," the two sisters grew very close, learned to be more patient with one another, and eventually became close friends.

After the group in hiding was discovered and sent to the concentration camps, Anne and Margot managed to remain together almost until the end. After surviving the Westerbork reception camp and the Auschwitz concentration camp, however, Margot became sick with typhus at the Belsen concentration camp in the winter of 1944–45. After being gravely ill and lying in a deep coma for days, Margot died at the end of February (or the beginning of March), 1945. While unconscious, she fell out of bed, and she was found dead when her friends tried to lift her back into her bed.

Otto Frank

The Franks were an old German-Jewish family. Otto Frank's father, a businessman, came from Landau in the Palatinate (a section of Germany). His mother's family can be traced in the archives of Frankfurt back to the seventeenth century.

Otto Frank was born and grew up in Frankfurt-on-Main and, after graduating from high school, went into business, like his father. He fought in the German army during World War I in an artillery company. He impressed his superiors and was promoted in the field to the rank of lieutenant.

After the war, he settled down in Frankfurt as an independent businessman, specializing in banking and the promotion of brand-name goods. He was a member of the comparatively prosperous middle class when he married Edith Holländer of Aachen. He was thirty-six years old, and she was twenty-five. In 1933, when Anne was four years old and Margot was seven, the family moved to Holland, following the rise of the Nazis to power and the introduction of harsh laws against all Jews in Germany. When Mr. Frank brought his family to Holland, he became managing director of an established firm and did well for seven years. When the Nazis invaded Holland in May 1940, however, they introduced the same anti-Jewish laws which had caused the Franks to leave Germany. Times became very difficult for the Franks, and Anne's father soon began to form a plan whereby they could "disappear"—that is, enter a hiding place that had been prepared in advance.

Otto Frank took his colleagues and employees at work into his confidence, and they all helped him prepare the upper rooms (at the back of the building where his business was situated) as a hiding place for his family. Items of furniture, bedding, and kitchenware—in fact, everything needed for a regular household—were taken there, little by little, so as not to arouse the attention or suspicion of anyone who was not a party to the pre-planned secret move. After the Franks had moved into the secret hiding place on July 8, 1942, a bookcase was attached to the door leading to the annexe so that the entrance was concealed. The "Secret Annexe" was a reality.

Throughout the two years that the Franks were in hiding, Mr. Frank was a pillar of strength for the group. It was he who tutored Anne, Margot, and Peter, it was he who always tried to soothe members of the group when tempers flared up and nerves were frazzled, and it was he who consoled and encouraged Anne and, presumably, the other members of the group, when the strain of being cooped up, in hiding, and under nightly bombardment became almost too much for them to bear. He readily shared his hiding place with another family, the Van Daans, and later on with another man, Mr. Düssel, even though this meant that the Franks' own living conditions were even more cramped and their food rations far more limited than before.

When the Nazis discovered the hiding place, all the members of the group, together with the two business associates who had been helping them, Mr. Koophuis and Mr. Kraler, were taken to Gestapo headquarters. Mr. Frank told Mr. Koophuis how bad he felt, knowing that his friend was being imprisoned for helping him. Mr. Koophuis told him not to give it another thought, that it had been his decision and he would not have done anything else. The group traveled together, without their Gentile helpers, by train to the reception camp at Westerbork. Although conditions there were bad, the families were still together, so their spirits were not too low. They knew the possibility of deportation to Poland existed, and they were aware of what happened at Auschwitz, Treblinka, Maidanek, and other concentration camps. On the other hand, they knew that the Allies were advancing and that the Russian Army was already deep in Poland, so that if luck were on their side, they *might* survive until the war was over.

Although the sexes were housed in separate barracks at Westerbork, Mr. Frank was able to visit his wife and daughters in the women's barracks. His presence was reassuring, and when Anne fell sick, he came over every evening, stood beside her bed for hours and told her stories. After being kept in the Westerbork camp for a few weeks, the Franks, the Van Daans, and Mr. Düssel were herded into a shipment of one thousand persons and sent to Auschwitz. This was the very last shipment to leave Holland. The people traveled in crowded, sealed cattle cars for three days and nights. At Auschwitz, men and women were separated, and that was the last Mr. Frank ever saw of his family.

When the SS guards left Auschwitz in January 1945, in order to escape the approaching Allies, they took most of the inmates of the camp with them, forcing them to march through the countryside barefoot, in rags, and without proper food. Mr. Frank was in the camp infirmary, and so he was spared. He was in Auschwitz when it was liberated by the Russians in February.

After the war, Mr. Frank returned to Holland via Odessa and Marseilles on board the New Zealand ship *The Monaway*, which brought concentration camp survivors from East to West Europe. He contacted the people who had helped him and his family while they were in hiding in Amsterdam, and Elli and Miep (as noted above) handed over to him the papers in Anne's handwriting which they had found on the floor of the "Secret Annexe" the day the Gestapo had come and taken the group away.

Otto Frank, as described by the writer Ernst Schnabel, was: ". . . a tall, spare man, highly intelligent, cultured and well-educated, extremely modest and extremely kind. He survived the persecutions, but it is difficult and painful for him to talk on the subject, for he lost more than can be gained by mere survival."

He survived until he was in his nineties and died in Amsterdam in 1980.

Mrs. Frank

Mrs. Frank was born Edith Holländer, and her family came from Aachen, a town on Germany's western border, near Belgium. Like her husband, she came from the comfortable middle classes and was accustomed to a life of relative ease, with most of the work in the house being done by servants. Her husband was eleven years older than she was, being thirty-six to her twenty-five when they were married in 1925. They lived in Frankfurt-on-Main, Germany, and their daughters, Margot and Anne, were born in 1926 and 1929, respectively. When the Nazis came to power, in 1933, and the persecution of the Jews of Germany began, the Franks moved to Holland.

For seven years, the Franks lived peacefully and prosperously in Amsterdam, but things changed when the Nazis invaded and occupied Holland in 1940. The Franks tried to continue living a normal life under the Nazi regime, but this became increasingly difficult, and in the summer of 1942, they went into hiding.

In the "Secret Annexe," Mrs. Frank was obliged to perform various tasks which she had not formerly been accustomed to doing. In addition, she was living in cramped quarters, together with her family and another four people. This obviously was not easy for her, and possibly much of the bad feeling between Anne and her mother may have been due to this and the effect that the cramped living conditions had on everyone's nerves.

After her arrest, Mrs. Frank was taken with her family to Gestapo headquarters in Amsterdam and the Westerbork reception camp. There, according to an eyewitness, she was very quiet. "She seemed numbed all the time. . . . Edith Frank could have been a mute. She said nothing at work, and in the evenings, she was always washing underclothing. The water was murky and there was no soap, but she went on washing, all the time."

Like the other members of the group, Mrs. Frank was included in the last shipment of people to be sent to Auschwitz from Holland in early September 1944. At Auschwitz, she was still with Anne and Margot, though separated from Mr. Frank.

On October 30, 1944, there was a "selection" among the women at Auschwitz, and the younger and healthier ones were sent on to the Belsen concentration camp. Anne and Margot were included in this group, while Mrs. Frank was left behind. The events which she had been through, the hunger, and the privation, had unhinged her mind, and she refused to eat. She began collecting what few crusts of bread she could find and hiding them in her bed, saying that they were for her husband. The bread spoiled, but still she continued to hoard it, unwilling or unable to eat. She was forty-five years old when she died in her bed in Auschwitz on January 6, 1945, ten days before the SS guards fled from the camp.

Mr. Van Daan

A business associate of Otto Frank's, Mr. Van Daan was, as someone who knew him put it, "a highly intelligent and well-bred man, but in time his nervous strength gave out." This is supported by Anne's account of him in her diary; his wife appears to have been the more domineering of the two, at least during the period while they were in hiding.

Once the group was discovered, like the rest, Mr. Van Daan was taken first to Gestapo headquarters in Amsterdam for questioning, and then he was sent to the Westerbork reception camp. He, too, made the long journey by train to Auschwitz, and once there, he was separated from his wife, whom he never saw again.

Mr. Van Daan was gassed at Auschwitz, and he was seen by Mr. Frank marching to the gas chamber together with a group of other men. The exact date is not known.

Mrs. Van Daan

Mrs. Van Daan was described by one of the group of Dutch "protectors" as: ". . . a very uncomplicated person, anxious and cheerful at the same time, as temperamental people often are." Anne's account of her in her diary is generally unflattering and intolerant, and we often feel that there was a great gulf of character and intelligence between them. What is evident is that Mrs. Van Daan was not a stoical person who shines in adversity.

Mrs. Van Daan was included in the last group of one thousand prisoners sent from Westerbork in Holland to Auschwitz in Poland on September 2, 1944, as the Nazis retreated before the advancing Allies. At Auschwitz, she was separated from her husband and son. She was sent to Belsen, separately from Anne and Margot, who were surprised to meet her there later on. It was she who heard Anne's friend, Lies, calling from another part of the camp, and who summoned Anne to their meeting.

Mrs. Van Daan died at Belsen, although it is not known whether she was gassed or succumbed to hunger or disease. The date of her death is not known, although it must have been after February, when Anne and Lies saw one another for the last time.

Peter Van Daan

One of the Dutch "protectors" has described Peter as a ". . . simple, lovable boy, whom Anne would sometimes tease for his slow, methodical ways." It is clear from Anne's diary that she loved him, although it is possible that she loved her dream of love rather than the boy himself. Peter was a quiet, handsome boy with a forest of brown curls and blue-gray eyes.

At the Westerbork reception camp, Anne and Peter were still together, and they made a striking and handsome pair. At Auschwitz, however, men were separated from women upon arrival, so we must presume that after their dispatch there, on September 2, 1944, they did not see one another again. When the women were ordered to go to the left, at the Auschwitz railway station, Peter, Mr. Frank, Mr. Van Daan, and Mr. Düssel had to turn to the right.

Peter was taken along by the SS guards when they left Auschwitz in January 1945. Mr. Frank, who was in the infirmary at the time, tried to persuade Peter to hide there too, but Peter did not dare to do so. It was bitterly cold and the roads were covered with ice as thousands of prisoners marched out of the camp, together with their guards. Many died of the cold, of hunger, and of exhaustion, and many were shot by the SS guards for lagging behind. Most of them were never heard of again. Peter Van Daan was among these.

Mr. Düssel

Mr. Düssel, the elderly dentist who joined the group in hiding in November 1942, had formerly lived in Berlin and was married to a Catholic woman. He and his wife emigrated to Holland after the anti-Semitic riots of November 1938 which took place throughout Germany.

When Mr. Düssel went into hiding, his wife was informed that he had managed to get out of the country, so she never knew that her husband was in Amsterdam, near her, until the group was discovered by the Nazis. The information was conveyed to her then by a member of the Dutch group of "protectors."

Life in the confined quarters of the "Secret Annexe" had made Mr. Düssel rather difficult, and Anne describes him with great severity in her diary. If life in hiding was uncomfortable and annoying, it was much more so if one had to share one small room with a somewhat pedantic, older man. The experience obviously was not a pleasant one for either Anne or Mr. Düssel.

Mr. Düssel went with the other members of the group first to Westerbork and then to Auschwitz. He was later separated from the other men in the group and was sent back to Germany. He died at the Neuengamme camp.

Lies (pronounced "Lees")

In her diary entry for Saturday, November 27, 1943, Anne writes: "Yesterday evening, before I fell asleep, who should suddenly appear before my eyes but Lies! I saw her in front of me, clothed in rags, her face thin and worn. Her eyes were very big and she looked so sadly and reproachfully at me that I could read in her eyes: 'Oh, Anne, why have you deserted me? Help, oh, help me, rescue me from this hell!' And I cannot help her, I can only look on, how others suffer and die, and can only pray to God to send her back to us."

Lies' father, who had been press chief of the last pre-Nazi administration in Prussia, had emigrated to Holland with his family in 1933. They lived near the Franks in a suburb of Amsterdam, and Anne and Lies went to school together and were good friends. Together with Anne, Lies had to leave the Montessori school and attend the Jewish school, wear the yellow star on her clothes, and have her movements increasingly restricted by the edicts of the Nazi authorities after 1940. The Jewish children, however, continued to go to school, meet their friends for ice cream, conduct themselves as normally as they could, and lead as carefree a life as possible under the circumstances. Their parents, and the Dutch population, did all they could to protect them from the harsh reality of life under the Nazis, until this was no longer possible.

Lies and her parents did not go into hiding because Lies' mother was expecting a baby. Relations in Switzerland had obtained South American passports for the family; thus, they hoped that they could remain unmolested. Nevertheless, they were sent to Westerbork in 1943, and later to the Belsen concentration camp. There, they lived in a block for "neutral foreigners," and they were occasionally permitted to receive a Red Cross package. Lies' mother died, and later, in the winter of 1944–45, Lies' father fell ill and died also.

The same winter, Lies heard that in the next block of the camp, which was separated from hers by a barbed wire fence, a group had arrived from Auschwitz, and that among the prisoners were Margot and Anne Frank. Lies waited until night, then stole out of the barracks, went over to the barbed wire fence, and called softly into the darkness: "Is anyone over there?"

As chance would have it, the voice which answered her belonged to Mrs. Van Daan, whom both Lies and the Franks, of course, knew, and it was she who went and called Anne. Both Anne and Lies were very weak and emaciated by then and simply cried upon seeing one another across the barbed wire fence. They told one another what had happened to their families, but Anne did not know where her father was, only that her mother had stayed behind in Auschwitz. She also told Lies that Margot was still with her, but that she was very ill.

Lies tried to get a little extra food and clothing across the fence to Anne, and she succeeded, in part. But this, it seems, was not enough to save Anne from the typhus that was raging in the camp, and from which Margot died a few days before Anne herself perished.

Lies was told that Anne had died of typhus, and she believes this because she never saw her after the February night when she attempted to throw a package across the wire fence to her. Lies was sent out of Belsen in a shipment destined for Theresienstadt, but their train traveled right into the middle of a Russian offensive, and the Russians liberated the prisoners. Today, Lies is a mother and housewife and lives in Jerusalem, Israel.

A woman who was in the camps at that time has said: "In Auschwitz we had had visible enemies: the gas chambers, the SS, and the brutality. But in Belsen we were left to ourselves. There we had not even hatred to buoy us up. We had only ourselves and our filthy bodies; we had only thirst, hunger, and the dead, the corpses lying all around, who showed us what a little thing life is. There it took a superhuman effort to remain alive. Typhus and debilitation – well, yes. But I feel certain that Anne died of her sister's death. Dying is so frightfully easy for anyone left alone in a concentration camp."

Mr. Kraler

After Mr. Van Daan's withdrawal from his firm, Mr. Kraler took over the management of dealings between Travis, Inc. and the affiliated firm of Kohlen and Co. He was an Austrian by birth, fought in the Imperial Navy during World War I, and he moved to Holland afterward. He was a business associate of Mr. Frank, whom he met in Amsterdam in 1933. When Jews were no longer allowed to own business enterprises, Mr. Kraler took over those run by Mr. Frank and Mr. Van Daan. This alone involved a certain amount of risk, as under the Nazi regime even the fact that they had formerly been Jewish-owned made them liable to be confiscated.

Mr. Kraler helped the Franks to prepare the "Secret Annexe" as a hiding place. While the group was in hiding, he was instrumental in obtaining supplies, keeping them secret and providing moral and psychological support. He was in the downstairs office when the police came to take the Franks, the Van Daans, and Mr. Düssel away. They asked Mr. Kraler for the owner of the house, and he gave them the name and address of their landlord. They insisted that they wanted the person in charge there, and when he said that it was he, they ordered him to come with them as they searched the building.

The police were acting on information passed to them by an informer, possibly one of the workers in the warehouse, and they would not allow Mr. Kraler to put them off the trail as they approached the bookcase which hid the door leading to the "Secret Annexe." And so, Mr. Kraler was the first one to ascend the steps, a pistol held against his back; he entered the Franks' room, where Mrs. Frank was standing at the table. He said, "The Gestapo is here," and Mr. Frank did not start in fright or say anything. The police gave the group in hiding enough time to collect a few possessions, then they, together with Kraler and Koophuis, were taken to Gestapo headquarters for questioning.

Because the year was 1944, and not 1943 or 1942, the Gestapo was more careful in its treatment of non-Jewish prisoners. It was evident by then that the Nazis would lose the war, and so, instead of treating them strictly and sending them to one of the death camps, they were treated more leniently. Mr. Kraler, like Mr. Koophuis, did not attempt to defend himself; he remained silent, and the officials obviously did not think it worthwhile to force them to talk.

Mr. Kraler was sent to a camp near Amersfort in Holland, and from there to a forced-labor camp in Zwolle. In March 1945, the inmates of the Zwolle camp were supposed to be removed to Germany. Four hundred men were marched under guard along the highway from Arnhem to Zevenaar. During the march, the column was strafed by planes, and in the confusion Kraler and another man managed to escape. They crawled off into the underbrush, and when the firing stopped, they slipped into a house. After an hour, they ventured out again and hid with a farmer for two days. Traveling by night over back roads, Kraler made his way to Hilversum, where his relatives lived. After the war, he moved to Canada.

Mr. Koophuis

Mr. Koophuis had met Mr. Frank in Amsterdam in 1923, when they both had business dealings there. This association continued intermittently until 1933, when the Franks moved to Amsterdam and the business relationship and personal friendship between the two men grew. In 1941, Koophuis took over Mr. Frank's place in the Travis company – otherwise, the firm would have been confiscated or liquidated as a Jewish business. It was Koophuis, together with Kraler, who proposed that the Franks use the back of the business building as a refuge. They helped the Franks move furniture and household items there, by stealth and at night, in order to avoid detection.

When a postcard reached the Franks in 1942, ordering Margot to report to the reception center at the Westerbork camp, everyone knew that the time to act had finally come. Mr. Koophuis was instrumental in ensuring that the secret of the group in hiding was kept, even though this raised many technical difficulties, particularly when the ownership of the building changed hands and the personnel in the warehouse also changed. Food had to be obtained for the group in hiding and paid for, extra food ration stamps had to be obtained, and in many cases, this aroused people's suspicions. Nevertheless, the baker, the vegetable man, and most of the other people with whom Koophuis had dealings, did not ask embarrassing questions; they simply cooperated in silence.

Mr. Koophuis has described the arrest by the Gestapo in the following words: "It was a Friday, and a fine August day. The sun was shining; we were working in the big office, Miep, Elli, and myself, and in the warehouse below us the spice mills were rumbling."

While Mr. Kraler accompanied the police in their search of the building, Mr. Koophuis and the two girls were ordered to remain at their desks. His first concern was to protect the two girls, and he told them to leave the building and insist that they had been unaware of what was going on, if asked. He was taken with the others to Gestapo headquarters, but largely because of his presence of mind, Miep and Elli were not taken too.

As they left the building, Mr. Koophuis relates: "I was the first to step out on the street. People were standing around on the sidewalk, staring as if there had been a traffic accident. They all looked stunned. I was also the first to get into the van and sat down way up in front, behind the driver."

As they waited in the cell at Gestapo headquarters, Mr. Frank told Mr. Koophuis how bad he felt that this had happened to them. Mr. Koophuis replied: "Don't give it another thought. It was up to me, and I wouldn't have done it differently." Koophuis and Kraler did not talk to their captors, who did not invest very much effort in forcing them to do so.

Fortunately, an international welfare organization intervened on behalf of Koophuis, pointing out that he was ill. He was released for medical care after a few weeks of imprisonment, and then he returned to Amsterdam.

Miep

Miep has been described by someone who met her after the war as "a small, delicate, intelligent young woman." She was born in Vienna, and she was sent to Holland after World War I as an "undernourished child" in whom a welfare organization had taken an interest.

She remained in Amsterdam, and in 1933 she met Mr. Frank, who hired her to work for the Travis company. When Austria was absorbed by Germany, she was given a German passport, and after the Germans occupied Holland, in 1940, she was asked to join a new club called "The German Girls Club in the Netherlands." She declined, stating quite bluntly that she did not want to join. A few days later she was summoned to the German Consulate, her passport was stamped as being invalid after three months, when she would have either to become a Dutch citizen or emigrate as "a stateless person."

At that time, Miep and Henk van Santen, a young Dutchman, intended to get married, and the situation created by the Nazis obliged them to move the date forward. There were various technical and bureaucratic difficulties, but in the end, with the cooperation of other Dutch citizens, Miep and Henk were married in July 1941, and Miep was legally able to remain in Holland.

Henk, like many Dutch people, worked in the Dutch underground resistance organization, which helped Jews and opponents of the Nazis hide from their oppressors. Miep and Koophuis knew or guessed what Henk was doing, but neither ever tried to stop him.

Throughout the period when Anne and the other members of the group were in hiding, Miep helped and encouraged them. She brought them food and visited them in their hiding place, bringing news from the outside and a breath of fresh air when she came. Anne longed for someone new to talk to, and Miep was a good friend to her. Together with Elli, she arranged little gifts and surprises on birthdays and festivals, brought wild flowers, and generally did her best to make the situation of the group in hiding a little more tolerable.

Miep and Henk even spent a night in the "Secret Annexe," because the children wanted "to have guests" so badly. It was a night of terror for them, however, and only the others slept soundly, having grown accustomed to the fear and discomfort.

When the police came to take the group in hiding away, Miep was in the office, together with Mr. Kraler, Mr. Koophuis, and Elli. They were all, except Mr. Kraler, ordered to remain where they were, while the search for the "Secret Annexe" was conducted. Mr. Koophuis tried to persuade Miep to leave, because it was obvious that they would all be arrested too, but she refused to go. Then Mr. Koophuis gave her the office keys and told her to insist that she had not known what was going on. "You can't save us," he said. "Save what can be saved. First and foremost, make sure that you are not involved."

Miep was in the office when the group in hiding went down the stairs, under police guard. She said, "I could hear the heavy boots, the light footsteps [of the others], and the very light footsteps of Anne. Through the years, she had taught herself to walk so softly that you could hear her only if you knew what to listen for. I had seen her only the day before, and I was never to see her again, for the office door was closed as they all passed by."

After the Franks and the others had been driven away in a police van, Miep was questioned by one of the policemen. She did as Mr. Koophuis had told her. She claimed that she had not known about the group in hiding. The policeman accepted her story, but told her to continue to come to the office every day, threatening that if she did not, her husband would be arrested and hinting that he knew about his resistance activities.

Henk and Miep sat up until late at night, discussing what action to take, but there was nothing they could do. When Miep was in the office the following day, one of the firm's traveling salesmen phoned, and Miep told him what had happened. He suggested that Miep try to bribe the police, and that she should do this quickly, while the prisoners were still in Amsterdam. He offered to contribute his own savings, and the baker from whom Mr. Koophuis had been buying bread for the group in hiding also offered to contribute something.

Miep went to Gestapo headquarters in Amsterdam a few days later and attempted to secure the prisoners' release for money but was told that although that had been possible in the past, that was no longer the case.

Today, Miep and Henk live in Amsterdam.

Elli

Elli was a young girl who worked in the office as a typist and was the closest to Anne during the period she was in hiding. She is a gentle, warm, shy person, and although she was eight or nine years older than Anne, she often discussed her personal problems with Anne. Elli also helped Anne and the others both practically and psychologically throughout the period they were in hiding.

Elli has said that Anne was sometimes bad-tempered and nasty, and at those times only her father, to whom she was very close, could bring her to her senses. He did it by saying the magic word, "Self-control!" This caused her to stop whatever it was she was doing and regain her composure.

Elli also spent a night in the "Secret Annexe," sleeping on an air mattress. This was in October 1942, and she claims that she did not sleep a wink that night and almost died of fright. The noises of the night, the bell of the clock tower nearby, and the fear of arrest or an air raid kept her awake all night. The other members of the group slept undisturbed, however.

When the Gestapo came to arrest the group in hiding, Elli became extremely distraught and cried like a little child. She stood at the window, crying and wringing her hands, while the police searched the house. Mr. Koophuis went over to her, gave her his briefcase, and told her to take it to the corner druggist, with a message that his brother would come and pick it up.

Elli made an immense effort to do as she was told and got to the druggist's store. She made up a story about their having been found possessing a radio set (they were illegal under the Nazi regime), and the druggist believed her. He took the briefcase and promised to give it to Mr. Koophuis' brother when he came. Elli then called Mr. Koophuis at the office and asked him what she should do, although she could hardly talk. Mr. Koophuis told her to go home, but she started crying again, and eventually remained with the druggist, crying and praying, for over an hour.

This is Elli's account of the events of that afternoon: "All afternoon I wandered through the city, not knowing where I was going, and did not reach home until dusk. My father was in bed. He had been operated on some time before. But when the doctors saw that he had cancer of the stomach, they could do nothing for him.

"I sat down beside his bed and told him everything. He was deeply attached to Mr. Frank, whom he had known a long time. He said nothing. But then he suddenly asked for his clothing, dressed and went away. When he came back after dark, he said there was nothing to be seen, that the building looked just as it always had. He had peered into the windows for awhile, but everything was deserted and still."

Today, Elli lives in Holland, together with her husband and children.

ESSAY TOPICS

1. Try to keep a diary for a week. Can you make it interesting and varied?

2. Imagine that you are in hiding with your family. Write descriptions of everyone's character, your feelings, conversations you have, and things you do.

3. What kind of a girl do you think Anne Frank was? Describe her character.

4. What do you think makes Anne's diary interesting?

5. What would you do if laws were passed against you because of, say, the color of your hair, eyes or skin, your grades in school, or your height? How would you feel and react?

6. Which character of the group in hiding do you like best? Why?

7. Pretend that Anne survived the concentration camps. Write an account of what she did when she grew up.

8. What can ordinary people do to make sure that other ordinary people within their society are not persecuted?

SELECTED BIBLIOGRAPHY

BETTELHEIM, BRUNO. *The Informed Heart.* Glencoe, Ill.: Free Press, 1960.

BIRENBAUM, HALINA. *Hope Is the Last To Die.* New York: Twayne, 1971.

COHEN, ELIE A. *Human Behavior in the Concentration Camp.* New York: Norton, 1953.

FRANK, ANNE. *Tales from the Secret Annex.* New York: Washington Square Press, 1983.

FRANKL, VIKTOR E. *From Death-Camp to Existentialism.* New York: Farrar, Straus, 1958.

GINZBURG, EUGENIA SEMYONOVNA. *Journey into the Whirlwind.* New York: Harcourt, Brace & World, 1967.

GLATSTEIN, JACOB, and SAMUEL MARGOSHES. *Anthology of Holocaust Literature.* New York: Atheneum, 1973.

GOLDSTEIN, BERNARD. *The Stars Bear Witness.* New York: Viking, 1949.

HART, KITTY. *I Am Alive.* New York: Abelard-Schuman, 1962.

KLEIN, GERDA WEISSMAN. *All But My Life.* New York: Hill & Wang, 1957.

KUZNETSOV, A. *Babi Yar.* New York: Farrar, Straus & Giroux, 1970.

MANDELSTAM, NADEZHDA. *Hope Against Hope.* New York: Atheneum, 1970.

MANN, GOLO. *The History of Germany Since 1789.* New York: Praeger Publishers, 1972.

PAWLOWICZ, SALA. *I Will Survive*. New York: Norton, 1967.

RAPPAPORT, ERNEST A. "Survivor Guilt," *Midstream*, XVII, August – September, 1971, pp. 41-47.

SCHNABEL, ERNST. *Anne Frank: A Portrait in Courage*. New York: Harbrace Paperback Library, 1958.

THORNE, LEON. *Out of the Ashes*. New York: Rosebern, 1961.

UNSDORFER, S. B. *The Yellow Star*. New York: Thomas Yoseloff, 1961.

VRBA, RUDOLF. *I Cannot Forgive*. New York: Grove, 1964.

WEISS, RESKA. *Journey Through Hell*. London: Vallentine, 1961.

WIECHERT, ERNST. *Forest of the Dead*. New York: Greenberg, 1947.

WIESEL, ELIE. *Night*. New York: Avon, 1969.

——————. *A Beggar in Jerusalem*. London: Weidenfeld and Nicolson, 1970.

——————. *One Generation After*. New York: Avon, 1972.

——————. *The Oath*. New York: Random House, 1973.

NOTES

NOTES